COMMUNISM IN RUSSIA

Studies in European History

Series Editors: John Breuilly
                    Julian Jackson
                    Peter Wilson

Studies in European History
Series Standing Order ISBN 0–333–79365–X
(outside North America only)

You can receive future titles in this series as they are published by placing a standing order. Please contact your bookseller or, in case of difficulty, write to us at the address below with your name and address, the title of the series and the ISBN quoted above.

Customer Services Department, Macmillan Distribution Ltd
Houndmills, Basingstoke, Hampshire RG21 6XS, England

Communism in Russia

An Interpretative Essay

Richard Sakwa

palgrave
macmillan

First published 2010 by
PALGRAVE MACMILLAN

Palgrave Macmillan in the UK is an imprint of Macmillan Publishers Limited, registered in England, company number 785998, of Houndmills, Basingstoke, Hampshire RG21 6XS.

Palgrave Macmillan in the US is a division of St Martin's Press LLC, 175 Fifth Avenue, New York, NY 10010.

Palgrave Macmillan is the global academic imprint of the above companies and has companies and representatives throughout the world.

Palgrave® and Macmillan® are registered trademarks in the United States, the United Kingdom, Europe and other countries.

ISBN: 978-0-333-60679-7 paperback

This book is printed on paper suitable for recycling and made from fully managed and sustained forest sources. Logging, pulping and manufacturing processes are expected to conform to the environmental regulations of the country of origin.

A catalogue record for this book is available from the British Library.

A catalog record for this book is available from the Library of Congress.

10 9 8 7 6 5 4 3 2 1
19 18 17 16 15 14 13 12 11 10

Printed and bound in China

Contents

Contents

Editors' Preface

The Studies in European History series offers a guide to developments in a field of history that has become increasingly specialised with the sheer volume of new research and literature now produced. Each book has three main objectives. The primary purpose is to offer an informed assessment of opinion on a key episode or theme in European history. Second, each title presents a distinct interpretation and conclusions from someone who is closely involved with current debates in the field. Third, it provides students and teachers with a succinct introduction to the topic, with the essential information necessary to understand it and the literature being discussed. Equipped with an annotated bibliography and other aids to study, each book provides an ideal starting point to explore important events and processes that have shaped Europe's history to the present day.

Books in the series introduce students to historical approaches which in some cases are very new and which, in the normal course of things, would take many years to filter down to text-books. By presenting history's cutting edge, we hope that the series will demonstrate some of the excitement that historians, like scientists, feel as they work on the frontiers of their subject. The series also has an important contribution to make in publicising what historians are doing, and making it accessible to students and scholars in this and related disciplines.

JOHN BREUILLY
JULIAN JACKSON
PETER H. WILSON

Introduction

Few countries have had as dramatic a history as Russia's in the twentieth century. The country as such disappeared for some seven decades during the Soviet period, only to re-emerge at the end of the century. For seventy-four years from 1917 the country was ruled by a party that claimed to be building some version of communism. This book is an essay on the experience of communism in those years. It is not a history of Russia over the last century, and neither is it a full-scale analysis of communism. The aim of the work is to examine the origins of the communist idea in Russian political thought and practice, the various forms that revolutionary socialism took in the pre-revolutionary period, and the resistance to these ideas. The nature of the revolutionary socialist challenge will be discussed, together with an examination of why a particularly virulent form came to power in Russia in 1917. The debates within the new communist regime will then be analysed, together with the failure of the alternatives to Leninist closure. The experience of the revolutionary society will be revealed in the light of various theories of Stalinism and totalitarianism. The traumatic aftershocks following the period of high totalitarianism gradually gave way from the 1950s to the decline of regime viability. Perestroika (restructuring) under Mikhail Gorbachev between 1985 and 1991 succeeded in reviving the political order but the country soon lost its recognisably communist features, while the state in which communism had taken hold disintegrated. The final chapter will seek to place the communist experience in a broader historical perspective.

The focus is on the 'short' twentieth century, from 1914 (or 1917) to 1989 (or 1991), but this has to be seen in the context of what might be called the 'long' twentieth century, encompassing the Marxist revolutionary challenge to capitalism from some time in

1

the 1840s, the emancipation of the serfs in Russia in 1861 and the epochal consequences of Russia's incomplete character as a nation state and modern polity, the belated industrial revolution in Russia from the late nineteenth century, and the onset of a modernity that simultaneously saw the dissolution of old bonds of order while establishing new forms of social integration. The long twentieth century, moreover, was a century of war and revolution. The modern era of conflict began in certain respects with the Franco-Prussian war of 1870, which set in motion a chain reaction of European 'civil wars', taking on a global character, that was only exhausted in 1945. Interstate war was accompanied by an internal 'cold war' of class conflict within societies, announced in *The Communist Manifesto* of Karl Marx and Friedrich Engels in 1848. This burst out into an armed 'hot' war in the Paris Commune of 1871, whose model of societal self-organisation was eulogised by Karl Marx in his *The Civil War in France*. In the Commune workers assumed the management of the city and developed new forms of popular administration and accountability. The text influenced Vladimir Il'ich Lenin's thinking, notably in his *The State and Revolution* of 1917, on the possibility of the working class taking over the management of the common affairs of society. In power, however, the communist ideal of social self-management turned into a severely statist and heavily bureaucratised system, characterised by high levels of coercion. The communist revolution, both in anticipation and in practice, died of exhaustion in 1989–91, and thus it was indeed at this time that both the long and the short twentieth centuries ended. The communist collapse was accompanied by the accidental disintegration of the country that it had established, the Union of Soviet Socialist Republics (USSR). What comes after, and Russia's place in it, is still not clear.

This study is concerned with a number of key themes. The first focuses on the fundamental question: why Russia? Revolutionary socialism was born in western Europe, yet it entered social consciousness in Russia in a far more profound way than in any other country. Numerous contingent factors, together with objective processes, can help explain the communist seizure of power in 1917; but the preconditions for the ability of small group of revolutionaries, in the form of Lenin's Bolshevik party, to take control of the world's largest country remain a mystery. For some the answer lies in Russia's innate authoritarianism, with the autocracy of the tsars replaced by a communist despotism. For others the answer lies at a more spiritual level: Russia's inability to accommodate itself to the strictures of a 'bourgeois' social existence and its endless striving for some sort of transcendence of historical and social reality. A view prevalent in post-communist Russia blames the west for having pushed the country to launch a military offensive on the eastern front in spring 1917, following the overthrow of Tsar Nicholas II in February but before the new authorities in the Provisional Government could consolidate their power, and thus a power vacuum was created into which the Bolsheviks boldly stepped.

The religious philosopher Nikolai Berdyaev argued that communism was a new form of Russia's traditionally messianic character. At an abstract level there may be some truth to such a characterisation, but in the event Soviet communism destroyed the foundation of traditional Russian eschatology, the Russian Orthodox Church and its social basis in the peasantry, and communist messianism, with its vision of a world revolution as extolled by leaders such as Leon Trotsky, saw Russia as little more than a dispensable platform from which to transform the world. In practice 'communism in Russia' became a *sui generis* type of 'Russian communism', not so much *merging* with Russian traditions to create a syncretic social order as *interacting* with Russian realities while retaining its organisational and ideological identity; while 'Russia' in the abstract retained its own identity. The two strands remained separate, but endlessly interwoven in complex patterns, and that is why ultimately no sustainable new *Soviet* synthesis emerged. By the end of perestroika a powerful sub-strand of Russian national self-assertion, whose symbolic leader was Boris Yeltsin, radically diverged from the communist thread and in the end became the dominant one, and the anti-communist movement took control of the fate of contemporary Russia, although with many a wistful glance backwards.

A second theme is the profound *resistance* to revolutionary and communist ideas from the very earliest period. Nikolai Gogol's early radicalism gave way to a profound conservatism, Mikhail Dostoevsky criticised the revolutionary idea in his *The Devils*, and many an early Marxist, like Peter Struve, later repudiated the very idea of revolution. Above all, the *Vekhi* (*Landmarks*) collection of 1909 still represents perhaps the most powerful and moving critique of revolutionary socialist ideas ever penned. The volume brought together some of Russia's leading intellectuals, who asked why the idea of revolution had become so attractive to so much of Russia's intelligentsia. The resistance continued even within the communist movement, with the radical socialists Karl Kautsky and Rosa Luxemburg criticising Lenin's conception of Bolshevik power, together with numerous critical movements within the Bolshevik party itself, notably the Democratic Centralists in 1919–20. Criticism and resistance continued, although mostly in subterranean forms or in exile, notably in Victor Kravchenko's moving testimony *I Chose Freedom* [96]. Resistance took the form of organised dissent during the leadership of Leonid Brezhnev (1964–82), and then became a flood during perestroika, helping to bring down the regime. In other words, any account that seeks to portray Russian communism as a new form of traditional Russian authoritarianism needs to explain the high level of intellectual and practical resistance to maximalist communist idealism in the country.

The Russian revolution (already critiqued by the *Vekhi* group in 1909) was a broad movement but in late 1917 it was hijacked by a small group of extremists led by Lenin in the Bolshevik party, who then proceeded to destroy not only the 'bourgeois' social order and its nascent institutions in Russia, such as the rule of law and an independent public sphere, but also the emancipatory ideals of 'the Russian revolution' writ large, a movement that since 1825 had been struggling for constitutionalism, civic inclusion and spiritual revival, as Leo Tolstoy argued so movingly in his book *The Meaning of the Russian Revolution*. The Leninist conjuncture also undermined the possibility of a socialist public sphere, civil society and polity, populated by worker organisations, co-operatives, self-managing communes and peasant communities, new forms of social living and gender relations, and managed by self-governing soviets (councils), all of which proliferated from 1917. Instead a grey, bureaucratised, intensely coercive and highly centralised social order was imposed, which became increasingly socially conservative and ultimately completely dysfunctional. In short, the Russian revolution carried within it diverse aspirations and hopes for new forms of freedom, but in the event the Bolshevik seizure of power in October 1917 was as much a coup *against* the Russian revolution as its fulfilment.

The third issue is a more institutional one and deals with the nature of the communism that ruled over Russia for seventy-four years. In his comprehensive study of the rise and fall of the sixteen communist systems that came to power in the twentieth century, Archie Brown [20] defines communism as a power monopoly by a centralised party, the predominance of non-market relations in the economy, and an ideological commitment to the global achievement of the movement's utopian goals of creating a non-capitalist social order. These three elements lie at the heart of communism in Russia, and combined to create a centralised power system ruling over the polity and economy while proclaiming its commitment to the spread of the revolution. In very few systems, Brown notes, did the assumption of power by the communist movement actually allow popular control and the reduction of alienation. Instead, bureaucratic systems became entrenched and self-serving elites consolidated into what Milovan Djilas later called a 'new class' [38]. From the very first days of Bolshevik power the problem of the state in a socialist system was raised, together with the possibility of an alternative to the statism typical of 'actually existing socialism'. Why did the state substitute itself so intensely for civil society in this system, despite Marx's aspirations, voiced so forcefully in his *The Civil War in France*, that under socialism the people would transcend the division between state and society?

Marx had never given any details about how the state would 'wither away' under communism, and, indeed, his emphasis on economic centralisation inevitably entailed an enhanced role for the central bureaucracy. Instead, the political state was abolished; that is, the whole panoply of independent law, individual rights, and traditional forms of representation and accountability that had developed over the course of centuries in the west. At the same time, Leninist organisational principles, and in particular the effective fusion of the communist party with the state, stifled the space for any autonomous role for social movements or workers' organisations. As a result the Soviet state was imbued with a monolithic and hierarchical character accompanied by only the most rudimentary and instrumental forms of mass democracy. The lack of independent economic relations and the absence of a structured and autonomous role for law deprived autonomous activity of any systematic framework. The new power monopoly was most apparent in respect of relations between the state and society, but it also applied to the internal operation of Soviet-type systems, however much in practice their institutions were fragmentary and confused.

The great paradox of communist systems was indeed the monolithic power exercised over society accompanied by almost permanent internal chaos and factionalism dominated by personalised dictatorship. The capricious and malevolent leadership of Joseph Stalin from the 1920s to his death in 1953 was replicated in most other communist systems. A social order predicated on the working out of impersonal class and productive forces turned out to mimic the forms of rule of archaic despotisms, although wreathed in the rhetoric of class emancipation and communist party rule. Thus Nikolai Bukharin, one of the original Bolsheviks, aptly observed that Stalin was 'Genghiz Khan with a telephone'; backed up, we may observe, with progressive forms of legitimation and implemented through the services of a modern bureaucracy.

The fourth theme is the distinctive understanding of temporality in revolutionary communist thinking. Reinhart Koselleck notes the shift in the understanding of historical time. Before the eighteenth century temporality was seen as the repeated unfolding of eternal verities. 'All variation, or change, *rerum commutation, rerum converse*, was insufficient to introduce anything novel into the political world. Historical experience remained involved in its almost natural givenness, and in the same way that the annual seasons through their succession remain forever the same, so mankind *qua* political beings remained bound to a process of change which brought forth nothing new under the sun' [92: *41–2*]. He goes on to describe the new quality with which historical time was imbued as a result of the concept of 'revolution' becoming more than circularity but overthrow and transcendence through a process of civil war. Like the Committee of Public Safety under Maximilian Robespierre and his fellow Jacobins in 1793–4, communism in Russia was mesmerised by a belief in history. Communist systems were regulated by a type of 'revolutionary time', inspired by a distinctive teleology focused on the ever-receding horizon of 'communism'. This was a linear transition based on Hegelian ideas of dialectical transformation and transcendence, in which Marx's ideas of revolutionary change are steeped. This characterises Lenin's ideas from 1914, when he carried out a close reading of Hegel's *Science of Logic* in response to the collapse of the Second International (the successor of Marx's

First International, an attempt to bring together the international socialist movement), and thus 'rediscovered the dialectic' from other Russian revolutionaries. The classic Hegelian idea of contradiction was now complemented by an emphasis on transition in which not only would the malevolent features of the old society be negated, but the very act of negation represented transcendence. This negative logic created an abyss at the heart of communism in Russia into which democratic pluralism and individual rights disappeared. The Soviet Union by its own self-characterisation was a transitional state, with socialism defined as the intermediate period in the shift from capitalism to communism; and in this transitional period the ideals that would be achieved in the final state did not apply, and thus a moral and political void was created.

This imbued the Soviet Union with a peculiar temporality where actual events were considered part of the unfolding of a revolutionary process, and thus served only as preparation for a different sort of time, when communism had been achieved. This relieved the regime, in its own eyes, of moral responsibility for its actions, since whatever actual crimes were committed today were 'for the good of the cause' (the reality of which Alexander Solzhenitsyn described so well in a powerful novella with that title). The present is devalued and emptied of intrinsic legitimacy; the anticipated future deprives the actual present of ontological significance. This represented a fundamental repudiation of Kantian morality, in which each individual is valued and each social act is judged in its own terms and not by some superior logic. Instead, Bolshevism in power from the very beginning was characterised by highly coercive practices and a moral relativism in which, as Lenin put it to the second Komsomol (Communist Youth League) congress in 1920, anything that served the revolution was moral. The ideology of transition legitimated the application of extreme violence 'temporarily' to destroy the alleged enemies of the revolution – the capitalist blood-suckers, the petty bourgeois intelligentsia, various renegades and backsliders, including later within the Bolshevik movement itself – to allow the communist social order, cleansed from unhealthy elements (as in the French revolution, the biomedical analogy was prevalent and epitomised by the concept of the 'purge'), to be built. There was no independent basis for morality, or indeed for politics in general, but whatever served the communist revolution was tautologically moral and appropriate.

The collapse of communism was accompanied by the repudi-ation of Hegelian notions of transition in favour of attempts to restore the neo-Kantian impulse based on individual morality and the discourse of human and civil rights, and thus represented the repudiation of revolutionary time. The fall of communism in Russia was accompanied by a broader retreat from the progressive utopianism born in the Enlightenment, and thus the particular event in Russia to that degree had universal significance. In prac-tical terms, however, the transition out of communism in certain respects mimicked the transition in the other direction, and thus the problem of revolutionary time was not resolved. The myth of the 1990s, where the 'Bolsheviks of the market' are charged with applying revolutionary methods to create a market-based democracy [141], stands as a symmetrical bookend to the history of communism in Russia: the revolutionary logic of transition created the communist system, and a similar logic was applied to its destruction at the end of the century. Thus 'revolutionary time' is certainly far from being a uniquely Bolshevik characteristic, but under their leadership (as during Jacobin rule) it was experienced with particular intensity.

A fifth theme is the role of ideology, ideas and political debate. There has been a long discussion on the degree to which the belief system of Bolshevik leaders shaped their political actions or whether the ideology served as little more than a mask to cover the actions of a grubby and violent self-serving elite. The problem is indeed a stark one, since so much of the practice of Soviet communism appears to repudiate basic principles of socialism. For example, from the very first days communist leaders became accustomed to higher living standards than the rank and file, and a finely graded system of privileges was the key instrument in Stalinist practices of governance. The corruption accompanying this inequality was one of the fundamental issues that provoked thousands to dem-onstrate against the communist regime in its dying days from the late 1980s. It is in this context that this work distinguishes between 'communism in Russia', which indicates that communism as an idea and set of practices existed separately from Russia, and 'Russian communism', which is the communism that is derived from Russia itself. The distinction of course is to a degree artifi-cial, since for seven decades Russia and communism were bound together, but, as we shall see, the distinction remained valid and during the 'great retreat' in the final Soviet years the independent subjectivity of Russia emerged as the single most powerful force that extinguished the communist incubus.

The problem of ideology, however, is a much more complex one than the 'masking' analogy or any reductionist notion of simple instrumentality can convey. We argue that the tension between beliefs and actions corresponds to the distinction between a core and an operating ideology. The core ideology consists of a number of propositions that were irreducibly drawn from the classics, and as long as the systems remained loyal to them the system could be considered communist. These include the common ownership of the means of production, some sort of commitment to a non-capitalist order, certain inclusive principles encompassing primarily class but also nationality, and a participatory ethos, however vitiated in practice. Marx had always argued that communism was not a set of principles to be implemented but something that would be devised in practice, a view that distinguished his programme from that of the Utopian socialists. This left a lot of scope for the core ideology of Marxism to be reinterpreted, and opened the door for communist rulers to apply a modified version, adapted to the immediate challenges. This danger quickly became apparent following the Bolshevik seizure of power, since there was only a vague Marxist standard against which the actions of communism in power could be measured. This allowed the Russian communists to assert that socialism was whatever they said it was, and an operating ideology quickly took shape. For seven decades the Russian leadership was able to leverage its position as the first, and for a long time the only, socialist state to become the arbiter of ideological principle – until challenged by Mao Zedong and the Chinese communists from the 1950s, and various other forms of heterodox communism, notably the 'self-managing socialism' practiced in Yugoslavia from the 1950s. The core and operating ideologies in the Soviet Union were flexible enough to ensure that, in the main, they did not come into open opposition. They existed along a spectrum in which different aspects could be highlighted when appropriate; but, at the same time, both retained distinguishing characteristics.

The operating ideology allowed endless compromises with the realities of holding on to power and to maintaining the status of the Soviet Union, along with its revolutionary ideology, in international affairs. Thus even the Nazi–Soviet pact of August 1939, which paved the way for the start of the Second World War, can be seen as an instance of the necessary flexibility endowed by the operating ideology to allow the continued existence of the core ideology. The relationship between the two is absolutely crucial, and it is the sphere in which the endless compromises that are part of being in government are devised. From the 1990s the political systems in China and Vietnam, and increasingly in Cuba, were no longer communist in terms of the operating ideology of market-driven modernisation governed by a communist elite. There, as in the Soviet Union, the core ideology was not abandoned, since that would have undermined the fundamental legitimacy of the regimes. New bases of legitimacy have emerged, with a shift to national economic development becoming central in Soviet Russia and later in China, but this was couched in the language of the core ideology, whose influence was far from negligible however much the practices of the operating ideology may have extended the bounds of the pragmatic end of the spectrum. In the end, of course, the predominance of the operating ideology in China and elsewhere will become so salient as to occlude even the residual elements of the core ideology; and the states will no longer be recognisable as communist. Communism will simply have become the form in which the societies modernised themselves. Communism in Russia, however, was not fated to have such an evolutionary outcome where the system adapts to global challenges and societal needs, and instead ended in a catastrophic breakdown.

This brings us to the final theme, the relationship between social development and political change. This concerns not just the philosophy and politics of civil society, but the 'materialist' understanding of the development of productive forces and shifts in class relations in response to technological and economic development. Materialist approaches to the analysis of historical development are far from being a Marxist preserve, although in studying the Soviet Union and its fall idealist approaches, paradoxically, have taken a firm hold. In other words, the fall of the USSR is often couched in terms of the struggle for human freedom and the triumph of a Kantian approach to morality, which insists on the value of every life, espoused by the underground human rights movement. At the same time, Soviet industrialisation clearly transformed Russia and, in creating a modern society, undermined the archaic principles of rule practised by the Communist Party. Changes in Russian society and in the global economic system, in the organisation of managerial hierarchies and labour, and much more, interacted with the development of ideas in the struggle for socialism and later for democracy in Russia. In both the creation and destruction of communism in Russia there was no simple deterministic logic at work. The problem of civil society in many respects undermined Marx's view that 'being determines consciousness'; the experience of the USSR demonstrates the role that consciousness and agency play in determining historical outcomes, but they do not do so in a vacuum.

A people socialised for three generations in communist ideology in the end revolted against the tutelage of the communist order. In part this was a response to material factors, notably the evident inability of the Soviet Union to provide living standards comparable to those in the west, accompanied by gross political and social inequalities; but it also reflected the aspirations to achieve those freedoms and civic dignity to which the Russian revolution had aspired for so long before 1917. Thus Kant's idealism was vindicated against Marx's materialism. The emergence of critical thinking in the heart of the regime and a widespread passive dissent indicated that one of the great lessons of the experience of communism in Russia is that the 'human factor', the term used by Gorbachev during perestroika, in great projects for social amelioration remains central. An irreducible aspiration to freedom in the end meant that Orwell's dystopian vision of the future presented in his *1984* had a sequel which we can label *1989*, the year of the great anti-revolutionary movements that not only brought down the oppressive and incompetent authoritarian systems of actually existing socialism, but also repudiated the logic on which they had been based. The great retreat in Russia was in these terms not simply a long-delayed 'counter-revolution' to the Bolshevik seizure of power, but represented a more profound 'anti-revolution' that transcended the two centuries of progressive philosophy in which it had been embedded. Whether this prepares the space for an improved and more pluralistic socialism or another type of emancipation is a matter of opinion, but any attempt to develop such a post-communist movement will have to come to terms with the experience of communism in Russia, and this book is a modest contribution to that debate.

This book makes no claim to be a full history of communism or of Russia. Instead it is an interpretative essay, raising certain questions about the nature and dynamics of communism in Russia, drawing on the major debates of our era while indicating some of the remaining controversies. Developments in the non-Russian republics of the Soviet Union are not covered. As it is an essay, only the most fundamental materials on which I have drawn directly will be referenced, although I acknowledge that I have drawn on a far greater body of scholarship in the preparation of this work.

1 Russia and Revolution

Following the defeat of Napoleon in 1815 the armies of the Russian tsar reached Paris. The military triumph was followed by hopes for constitutional reform at home as the ideas that had inspired the French revolution filtered back to Russia [110]. The Decembrist uprising in 1825 signalled the beginning of a revolutionary movement for political change: the Russian revolution had begun. The partial and disappointing land reform of 1861 and the continued blockage on political reform that could ensure effective and meaningful popular participation and the rudiments of executive accountability inspired an increasingly strong radical movement that looked to revolution as the solution to the country's problems. Quite why the siren call of revolution should have been so strong in Russia is still not clear. The classic Leninist formulation suggests that political and economic backwardness breeds radical solutions as a way of overcoming the resistance of the ruling elites. The argument undoubtedly contains an element of truth, but this is to formulate the problem in a Leninist way. While Russia certainly lacked the extensive civic traditions and increased popular representation that was developing in western European and the United States, the extent of Russian civic backwardness has been exaggerated by opponents of the old regime. In fact, on the eve of the political maelstrom of 1917 Russia was developing a complex civil society and extensive forms of civic engagement. This was a race between the evolutionary development of a more robust and hegemonic *ancien regime* and a militant revolutionary movement, with liberal reformers and moderate revolutionaries in between. The onset of war in 1914, however, polarised the situation, and defeats on the battlefield and dislocation at home in the end gave victory to the most extreme revolutionaries.

The Russia question

There is a large literature, in Russia and abroad, arguing that Soviet communism fits into a traditional pattern of Russian state–society relations. Robert Tucker put this best when he argues that, irrespective of changes in political regime, a certain view of the state has been relatively constant. He calls this the image of dual Russia: on the one side *vlast'* (power) or the state (*gosudarstvo*), encompassing autocratic power and bureaucratic officialdom; while on the other there is the population at large, society (*obshchestvo*) and the people (*narod*). The division is more than descriptive but is fundamentally evaluative, with state power seen as something profoundly alien and hostile; with the implication, moreover, that it is of questionable legitimacy, to be tolerated at best but not something belonging to the people, a theme developed by Oleg Kharkhordin [84]. The creation of a centralised autocracy from the sixteenth century was in part a response to security threats, and the link remains between relatively autonomous state power at home and geopolitical challenges abroad. As Tucker notes, Russia expanded from 15,000 square miles in 1462 to one-fifth of the world's land surface in 1917, placing a premium on military strength [181: *123*]. With Peter I (known as 'the Great') in the early eighteenth century this alienation was reinforced by the imposition of a western-inspired modernisation model, with the state seen as a type of occupying force, and by 1917 it had few supporters left. A type of inner decay eroded support for the regime and undermined self-belief, a process paralleled at the end of the Soviet system. The revolution destroyed the old state, but in its place a much more savage and dictatorial system was built, which nullified 'sixty years of Russian history in emancipating society from the aegis of the state' [185: *132*].Under Stalin *gosudarstvo* once again waxed strong, and the legacy of the radical estrangement of power and people has not yet been transcended.

A different form of determinism is based on interpretations of Russian political culture. For Edward Keenan [81] in his 'Muscovite Political Folkways' the consolidation of the Stalinist system in the 1930s represented a return to the tradition of Muscovite political culture. In his view, the late nineteenth and early twentieth centuries had been an aberration when Russia was beginning to adopt modern, western-style ideas and methods, but this was not destined to last. The Muscovite culture before 1700, in his view, operated at three social levels: the peasant culture, the culture of the court, and the bureaucratic culture. In the past they had operated separately, but in the modern period merged. All three operated in informal ways bound not so much by political institutional rules as by birth, personal affiliation and other traditional ascriptive relationships. This was a culture that sought to avoid risk, had no notion of progress, and subsumed the individual in the collective life of the particular subculture. Communist rule, from this perspective, represented not the cultural modernisation of Russia but the perpetuation in new forms of traditional patterns and the repudiation of the genuine modernisation that was taking place at the turn of the century. For Keenan, Nikita Khrushchev (who succeeded Stalin in 1953) sought to break out of the Muscovite–Soviet tradition to restore the ruptured modernising tradition. He hoped to do this by decentralisation and allowing the development of a sphere of public discussion, policies to be safeguarded by détente with the west. In practice, it was not so much Khrushchev who restored a public sphere and elements of governmental accountability, but rather Gorbachev and his programme of 'reform communism', which in the end challenged the system to become a 'communism of reform', containing within itself the potential to transcend communism itself – a process that was taken to its logical conclusion in China later.

The state was considered above society to perform tasks of national importance, and the system was never intended to be responsive to popular demands. However, this is a rather one-sided interpretation. The development of forms of self-governance in Novgorod and Pskov in the early modern era suggests that the view of Russian history as the unbroken history of a dominant state should be modified [125]. However, the tradition of popular government, notably through the *Veche* (civic assembly) in Novgorod, was crushed by Ivan the Terrible in the sixteenth century. While Russia did have a strong bureaucratic tradition, rationalised by Peter the Great, the tsarist bureaucracy was tiny compared with that of the Soviet state. There are continuities in bureaucratic culture, but there was not only a quantitative but also a qualitative difference between the two.

Tensions between state and society of the 'dual Russia' sort were only one facet of the 'Russian problem', and relations between the state and nation have still not been satisfactorily resolved. Liberal pre-revolutionary Russian historians argued that Russia was a state and not a nation, and certainly the country developed as an empire rather than a nation state [72]. Not only did the Russian state stand above society, but the state itself had distinctive 'imperial' characteristics. The emergence of a state separate from the institutions of the monarchy is part of the struggle for the emergence of a modern differentiated society, but in tsarist Russia the development of this sort of modern state was stunted. One consequence was the relative weakness of ethnocentrism, with little attempt to ensure the congruence of national and political borders. Another was the underdevelopment of a specifically national consciousness, which only reinforced the exaggerated stress on the Russian concept of statehood.

A further feature was the relatively large role played by the state in economic development. Alexander Gerschenkron [55] stressed the role of the state as initiator of economic activity in a cyclical pattern. Russian territorial expansion brought it into conflict with western powers, which required the modernisation of the relatively backward economy, and this was undertaken by the state for military reasons. Rapid growth was achieved by often brutal means in a short period of time, as under Peter the Great, Sergei Witte in the 1890s and Stalin in the 1930s, leaving the country exhausted once victory was achieved. This was then followed by a period of recuperation and relative stagnation. Instead of being marked by what Joseph Schumpeter called 'creative destruction', the constant cycle of replacement and innovation in which, as Marx put it in the *Communist Manifesto*, 'everything that is solid melts into the air', Russian development was characterised by a profoundly conservative ethos that sought to preserve tradition for too long before the onset of a new cycle of revolutionary change. The tension between western-inspired models of development and Russian *samobytnost'* (native traditions) defines modern Russian history.

This is revealed most vividly in the following encounter. In 1773 Denis Diderot (1713–84), one of the foremost Enlightenment thinkers and chief editor and contributor to the *Encyclopédie*, spent five months in St Petersburg, and had numerous long conversations with Catherine the Great. As far as Diderot was concerned, it appeared that Catherine was quite happy to be 'enlightened', as long as this did not undermine her 'despotism'. Her comments on the various projects put forward by Diderot make equally fascinating reading [37]. She dismissed them as 'mere babble that shows neither knowledge of the subject nor discretion, nor insight'. In particular, in a famous reply she told Diderot: 'You, as a philosopher, work on paper, which will bear everything; whereas I, poor empress, work on human skin, which is far more sensitive' [186: 6]. The pathos of the meeting between Diderot and Catherine, between the Enlightenment and absolutism, between Europe and Russia, and between volition and tradition, universalism and particularism, is one that resonates across Russian history as foreign-inspired developmental models encounter Russian resistance that continues to this day. The idea of 'sovereign democracy' advanced by sections of the elite during Vladimir Putin's presidency is little more than a variation on an old theme.

The political manifestations of Russia's statism were remarked upon by all commentators. The observations of the Marquis de Custine, based on a thirteen-day visit to Russia in 1839, have enjoyed wide resonance to illustrate the cloying predominance of bureaucratic rule. For Custine, 'Government in Russia is military discipline in place of civil order, a state of siege which has become the normal state of society' [31: 44]. He considered Russia 'a mixture of Byzantine finesse and Asiatic ferocity' [31: 22], where 'the government rules everything and vitalises nothing' [31: 225]. Borrowings from the west were designed simply to perpetuate traditional forms of rule:

> Since Peter I, the problem confronting the rulers of Russia has been to take advantage of administrative progress in the European nations in order to govern sixty million people in the Oriental manner. The reigns of Catherine the Great and Alexander merely prolonged the systematic childhood of this nation which still exists only in name. [31: 102]

Custine's letters form the basis of a tradition of thinking about Russia that was brilliantly summarised by Tibor Szamuely in his *The Russian Tradition*. According to him, 'Most incomprehensible and alien of all, pervading and colouring every Western description of Russia, was the awesome sway of an omnipotent state exercising unlimited control over the persons, the property and the very thoughts of its subjects' [173: 8]. He proposed a variant of the 'frontier thesis', arguing that the absence of natural borders and a relentless cycle of invasions and repulsions, of occupation and colonisation, shaped the omnipotent Russian state.

Russia's geopolitical position, with 240 years of Mongol suzerainty (1240–1480) followed by a relentless cycle of imperial expansion across contiguous territory, certainly endows Russia with a pattern of state development that does not easily fit into European categories. A common feature of much Central European writing, typified in a seminal article by the Czech writer Milan Kundera [99], is the attempt to cast Russia out of Europe into a zone of its own, alien and threatening, while stressing their own Europeanness. An important strand in Russian thinking, of course, has done the same, though from the opposite perspective.

Perhaps the most striking feature of Russia as it entered the twentieth century was the absence of a single national community. This was evident in agrarian matters, with the gulf between what was called 'educated society' and the peasant world acknowledged by contemporary and later commentators. There was less agreement, however, over the nature and dynamics of change in the countryside. When it came to the peasant question, the liberal view echoed the Marxist argument that, as capitalism penetrated the villages, social differentiation increased. For Lenin, the ensuing class conflicts would bring into being a radicalised and impoverished section of the peasantry ready to overthrow the landlord system in its entirety. Liberals, however, looked to the emergence of a 'sturdy yeomanry', dubbed *kulaks* (rich peasants) in Russian, which would act as the vanguard of the modernisation of the countryside in a rural economy oriented to the market. The Populists would have none of this, in either the Marxist or liberal variant, and asserted, despite the enormous changes in the years since the emancipation of the serfs in 1861, that the social structure of peasant life remained stable and that its communal principles endured relatively intact. This was the basis for the programme of the Socialist Revolutionary (SR) party, which tried to devise a Russian path to socialism. The Populists, however, shared the Marxist and liberal view that 'change' and 'development' were of the essence, but only differed in the meaning and definition of this 'progress'. For the peasants themselves, however, the key values were stability and continuity, and, although increasingly engaged with the market, traditional communal principles remained strong, together with customary law [77].

The tension between an imperial state and the many peoples comprising the empire inhibited the development of what else-where came to be known as a 'nation state'. The supranational character of the bureaucracy and the army reinforced the gulf between the state and the people, with the person of the tsar the great symbolic linkage point. When the tsar was discredited, as Nicholas II was by 1917, there was little to keep the country together. Even the 'Russian' core of the empire was made up of a multiplicity of peoples, and the very definition of what constituted an ethnic Russian was unclear, as in certain respects it is to this day. The Ukrainians in the Russian empire were known as 'Little Russians', while the White Russians (Belarusians) were barely distinguished from their Great Russian brothers. The imperial dimension of Russia's political evolution did not only affect the political organisation of geographical space, but imbued its ruling classes with a 'civilisational' rather than a 'national' perspective. While messianic ideas about Russia's unique destiny may have been prevalent among certain parts of the elite [39], the more immediate challenge was how to convert a dynastic agglomeration into a functioning political community. Russia was engaged in precisely this great transformation in the early years of the twentieth century, accompanied by the greater autonomy of society, when the catastrophe of the Great War intervened in 1914.

On the eve

The great sociologist Pitirim Sorokin wrote of his childhood in Vyatka (Kirov) region before the revolution, noting that 'A *Gemeinschaft* [community] spirit of mutual aid was still vigorous in my time, manifesting itself in many forms of collective activities within the whole village community. These conditions prevented the development of discernible inequalities and sharp economic, political, and social stratification. ... As a result there was no "class-struggle" and no crystallised political parties of vested interests' [168: *15*]. These experiences led him to join the SRs, which unlike Marxists appealed to all labouring classes, peasants, workers and intellectuals. According to Sorokin, the party placed less emphasis on 'materialism and the economic interpretation of man and history' and instead was 'much more idealistic and integralistic'

[168: *44*]. Sorokin's work indicates how the Russian revolution was a swelling tide that in certain circumstances could have become hegemonic: that is, propelling the government towards accelerated evolutionary change that might have averted a violent revolutionary dénouement. In the event, with the onset of war this was not to be the historical outcome.

Subversive educational work among workers and peasants, Sorokin notes, was 'considered as the moral and political duty of every "critically thinking and morally responsible person", to use the popular expression of P. Lavrov, one of the leading ideologists of the Social-Revolutionary Party' [168: *71*]. In 1906 Sorokin was arrested as a result of his agitation among peasants, and spent a short time in gaol, which turned out to be 'much less painful and frightening than I had imagined'. In fact, his comments reflect a system in decline: 'During its last years the collapsing Czarist regime became quite humane. As a matter of fact, we political prisoners made the prison a safe place to store revolutionary literature and employed prison guards as liaisons with outside revolutionaries, freely visited one another, and, unhindered, met daily to discuss political, social, and philosophic problems' [168: *45*]. He wryly notes the Russian saying of the time that 'One takes a leave of absence in prison to do some reading, thinking, and writing' [168: *46*].

Sorokin's comment on the decay of the regime also applies to the Soviet system in its final days: 'When a political regime begins to crumble, the "viruses of disintegration" rapidly spread throughout its whole body, "infect" most of its anti-bodies, and penetrate into its deepest recesses. Its downfall is usually due not so much to the efforts of revolutionary leaders as to its senility, impotency, and uncreativity' [168: *45*]. Thus the Russian revolution was much bigger than the Bolsheviks, and the October revolution represented a coup *within* the revolution as *against* the old order. As a result, following the revolution for which he had worked so hard, Sorokin in January 1918 suffered incarceration at the hands of the Bolsheviks in the Peter and Paul fortress in Petrograd (as St Petersburg had been renamed in 1914), in far less congenial circumstances than under tsarism as he witnessed the practices of the Red Terror take shape.

It was the communal traditions described by Sorokin that were challenged by Pëtr Stolypin, prime minister of Russia from 1906 until his assassination in 1911. The October Manifesto of 1905 established a new political framework for Russia, with a semi-constitutional monarch ruling with a new bicameral parliament, the Duma and State Council. The gentry, who made up 1.5 per cent of the population, were greatly over-represented after June 1907 in the Duma, taking up 49 per cent of the seats. The peasantry comprised 84 per cent of the population, but after 1907 had only 22 per cent of Duma deputies. By an edict of 9 November 1906 Stolypin sought to free peasants from what he considered the shackles of communal landholding to allow the most dynamic to individualise their holdings as farmsteads, *khutora* or *otruba*. The scale and nature of the Stolypin reforms in the countryside remain a matter of considerable controversy. Who left the commune to take up outwork in the burgeoning industrial economy: the extremely poor or the rich who had freed themselves from communal ties? Or was it both, with the middle strata left in the villages to consolidate their property rights over land, but not necessarily separating out from the commune entirely, as desired by Stolypin? The reform developed as the interaction of governmental action and the peasantry in the process of its implementation. More broadly, Stolypin sought to integrate the peasantry into the mainstream of Russian society as equal citizens: 'The government's long-range objectives were to bring the Russian peasants into the state's political-legal order as full-fledged citizens and to remove traditional obstacles to the development of modern agriculture' [194: *292–3*]. The successful implementation of this programme would have brought the peasantry into the existing political community, thus thwarting the ambitions of those politicians who sought to build *Sonderweg* (own path) programmes of revolutionary renewal on the backs of the peasants [185].

Stolypin's strategy was based on the belief that the revolutionary challenge, which but for the loyalty of the armed forces threatened to bring down the autocracy in the 1905 revolution, could only be blunted by a comprehensive programme of reform. His vision, however, was not shared by the tsar, the State Council, government officials in the centre and the localities, or by the nobility, groups that allied to resist his reforms of the *zemstvo* system of local government. Despite attempts to ally with the liberals, the latter saw only his harsh response to the peasant uprisings of 1905–6 and his dissolution of the first two State Dumas in 1906 and 1907, and thus failed to provide critical support to the beleaguered 'authoritarian reformer'. Like Yuri Andropov, the former head of the secret police (KGB) turned reformer in his brief reign in 1982–4, Stolypin practised the well-known conservative motto that one needs to change a little to prevent large-scale change. Despite his ambivalent relationship with the tsar, Stolypin remained a supporter of the monarchical order; and, despite working well with the Third Duma from 1907, he did not entertain ideas of subordinating the government to legislative control. The working practices of the Duma itself inhibited the passage of reformist legislation, lacking a system to keep bills moving through parliament, quite apart from the political opposition of the gentry and bureaucracy itself. The institutional framework of government undermined his ability to pursue a coherent strategy – attempts by Witte to establish a conventional ministerial structure led by a prime minister with a proper coordinating role had been defeated. The strength of conservative resistance to Stolypin's various reforms, encompassing peasant landholding, local government, the legal system, civil rights, workers' insurance and religious freedoms, meant only a small part of his agrarian reform made it to the statute books, and well before his assassination Stolypin was politically marginalised and he turned to nationalist politics.

In a famous interview in 1909 Stolypin asserted that 'Give the state twenty years of peace both at home and abroad and you will then not recognise Russia' [171]. Stolypin represented perhaps the last opportunity for the monarchy to modernise itself and respond to the changes taking place in society. Stolypin was an unyielding monarchist, and is indeed remembered to this day as 'the last great defender of the autocracy', but his vision of a modernised monarchy was subverted by opponents in the court itself and encountered strong opposition from his political adversaries. With his death events in Russia became ever more conflictual and polarised, ultimately leading to the revolutions of 1917. The shooting of unarmed striking gold miners on the Lena River on 4 April 1912 by tsarist troops, acting on behalf of the mining company, signalled the conclusive unravelling of Stolypin's programme and heralded, as conventional historiography puts it, the start of a new revolutionary upsurge. Instead of bringing about a great Russia, the twentieth century became one of great disturbances for the country.

A recent study of the Lena shooting, however, argues that even that terrible event did not herald the fragmentation of tsarist society, as Leopold Haimson and many others have argued, and instead a model based on 'social consensus rather than fragmentation' is more convincing [114: *183*]. For many, especially in the post-Soviet period, Stolypin became the symbol of those who hoped for an internal evolution of the autocracy into some more constitutional form of governance. Contrary to much émigré historiography, written typically by socialists as critical of the tsarist regime as they were of the Bolsheviks, the goals of 'the Russian revolution' could have been achieved in an evolutionary manner.

The final years of tsarism were a 'silver age' in poetry and the arts in general. The 'World of Art' movement of the turn of the century had a profound impact on the aesthetics of Russian civilisation. Russian folk art and customs were reinterpreted by such artists as Boris Kustodiev, Nikolai Sapunov, Nikolai Roerich and Zinaida Serebryakova, and then brought before a world audience, as were Sergei Diaghilev's famous ballet Russian Seasons in Paris and other European capitals. The stage designs of Alexander Benois, Leon Bakst, Alexander Golovin, Mstislav Dobuzhinskii and others gave flesh to Russian 'pagan' myths, legends and fairy tales. But at heart the movement reinterpreted Russian culture as a whole, and imbued the Russian peasant and merchant class with a cloudless optimism that seemed to shrink from the gathering clouds of the revolution. In other words, the aesthetics of the movement challenged the harsh idealism of the revolutionaries with another ideal rooted in the reinvention and reinvigoration of national traditions.

The traditional image of Russia before 1917 as sunk into oriental despotism and a police state is inadequate and misleading. The 1905 revolution forced the creation of a constitutional monarchy, and the rudiments of parliamentary life were introduced. Of course, genuine political accountability was lacking, and the court was the seat of conspiracies and intrigues, epitomised by the nefarious role played by the monk Grigory Rasputin. This was balanced by the rapid development of what was called 'society' (*obshchestvo*) from the late 1800s, taking multifarious forms of civic activity and engagement with social problems. There were numerous voluntary associations, worker mutual provident funds, cultural and literacy circles and, after the 1905 revolution, trade unions. While civil society in pre-revolutionary Russia may not have been mature, it was certainly extensive and rather less 'gelatinous' than Antonio

Gramsci later suggested. In his famous words,

> In Russia the State was everything, civil society was primordial and gelatinous; in the West, there was a proper relation between State and civil society, and when the State trembled a sturdy structure of civil society was at once revealed. [63: *238*]

The lack of a 'powerful system of fortresses and earthworks' behind the state allowed the Bolsheviks to take power in October 1917, but these ramparts had already been weakened by three years of war and revolution.

While the tsarist state was too incoherent to be able to sustain a state-directed programme of social and political renewal, society itself was in the throes of powerful currents of change. There were major developments in the emergence of civil society, with greater popular autonomy and the growth in local competencies, above all through the *zemstvos*, in the municipalities and in the life of the professionals. Private entrepreneurship also played a greater role than the common wisdom would suggest, as demonstrated in Charles Ruud's biography of the entrepreneur and book publisher Ivan Sytin [149] and Peter Gatrell's analysis of private armaments' manufacturers [54], as well as studies of merchant Moscow [175]. Even among the working class it is clear that there was great heterogeneity, with a rapid process of upward social mobility, while numerous recent studies stress just how complex was the peasant's relationship with the land. The emergence of civil society before 1917 was far greater than is usually allowed.

This was accompanied by the growing self-confidence of major civic institutions, notably the universities, the law courts and professional associations, as well as the instruments of urban and rural local government. There had been a rapid increase in the number of students across the empire, which by 1913 reached 70,000. The circulation of newspapers greatly increased, together with the number of journal titles and their readership. In 1913 there were 575 publishing companies, which between 1900 and 1917 published 7,061 authors, and in 1915 no fewer than 235 literary–cultural journals were issued, of which 128 were in Russian – and this in a supposed 'backward' country. This was accompanied by vigorous debates in the public sphere, with the profound divisions in society reflected in the party system that had been generated by the needs of society itself. A democratic and pluralistic culture was certainly not lacking, although balanced by some deeply traditional institutions, notably the Orthodox hierarchy. Thurston [175] demonstrates the development of this 'society' on the basis of the city of Moscow. He shows how the Moscow bourgeoisie, an important section of which was rooted in Old Believer traditions, had developed inclusive 'hegemonic' policies, which sought to bring workers into the broader community. While St Petersburg society was characterised by a sharp gulf between workers and the bureaucratic and business elites, where international (primarily French) capital predominated, in Moscow a different 'national' capitalism developed, accompanied by inclusive 'hegemonic' strategies of rule.

Underlying all of these developments is the question of the source of authority in the polity. The tsarist system vested authority in the person of the monarch as the representative of temporal and secular power. The mental anguish endured by Nicholas II as the democratic and radical insurgents sought to extract ever greater concessions from him following the 1905 revolution was quite genuine. As far as he was concerned, the devolution of rights through such new-fangled monstrosities as constitutions and the rule of law would represent an abdication of his responsibility to preserve the monarchy as the embodiment of Russian statehood. Popular sovereignty as the source of authority was anathema to him, and he retained a stubborn belief in his God-given right to rule, although accompanied by a sense of responsibility for the fate of the country.

Jonathan Daly offers an unconventional study 'from the other side of the barricades' of the last years of the tsarist regime, analysing Russia's security police. Although the empire may have been ramshackle and its administrative system far from an ideal type of bureaucratic organisation, Daly [32] endorses Aleksandr Blok's view that the security police was Russia's only functioning institution. The administration worked remarkably well in the circumstances and achieved some notable successes, and indeed forced the revolutionaries on to the defensive for most of this period, but ultimately they were let down by a tsar and top leadership who were simply unable to comprehend the scale and, perhaps more importantly, the nature of the challenge facing them. It was not so much the revolutionaries who overthrew the old regime, but the educated public and mass protest. This was the great river of the Russian revolution seeking to transcend the gulf between *vlast'* and *obshchestvo* to create a single Russia.

The call of revolution and its critics

In the early years of the twentieth century Bukharin noted: 'I do think we have entered upon a period of revolution which may last fifty years before the revolution is at last victorious in all Europe and finally in all the world' [140: 54]. Why did the socialist revolution break out in Russia rather than in France or Germany, countries that by most indicators were more 'ripe' for Marxist revolution? In 1883 Georgy Plekhanov, one of the founders of the Marxist revolutionary movement in Russia, observed that for the process of socialism to be carried out successfully the appropriate economic conditions would have to exist. If they did not then violence would have to be used, or the country would have to focus on policies directed against socialism, in effect capitalism. A strange inversion of the Marxist revolutionary process occurred: for Marx socialism was meant to come after capitalism (although he allowed that in Russia other options were possible), but most twentieth-century communist revolutions have been revolutions not of development but of backwardness. The socialist revolution became the key to development and not its fulfilment. Communist revolutions, moreover, took place not in the core capitalist countries but in the peripheries of the world economy, not in Europe but in Asia and Africa. Russia, as a country with one leg in Europe and one in Asia, reflected these two facets of twentieth-century communism.

The communist revolution in Russia represented the high water mark of one of the most ambitious eschatological projects of modernity [153]. The Bolshevik revolution in October 1917 revolution was an epochal event, in the sense that it endowed a parochial disturbance with universal significance. The emergence during the eighteenth century of a discourse of progressive social change based on a universal model of rationality and development applicable to all societies was now implemented in a country that even during the Enlightenment had an ambiguous relationship with the new forms of modernity being devised at that time. As we have seen, this was vividly in evidence in the correspondence between Catherine the Great and Diderot. While the renowned Encyclopaedist flattered

Catherine in public, he expressed private reservations whether she had understood the progressive ideas that he and his fellow enlighteners were advancing; while Catherine in her letters clearly indicated that, while the ideas of freedom and perfectability were all very fine, Diderot and his associates did not understand the realities of Russian politics. Thus the tension that remains to this day was exposed between expansive ideologies claiming universal application and the particularity of the Russian tradition.

This ideology in the hands of some Enlightenment thinkers (but certainly far from all) was combined with a revolutionary approach to social change – that the act of rupture itself had a liberating and progressive political effect. For want of a better term, this can be called *Enlightenment revolutionism*: asserting an ideology of human betterment accompanied by the development of a method – revolution – to implement the idea. The Enlightenment thus created a new praxis: an ideology of universal transformation, and the method of political revolution. It is this ideology of universal progress against which John Gray has repeatedly inveighed as having opened the door to the fascist and communist dictatorships and the impoverishment of the human spirit [64]. His critique is powerful and convincing, although it should be noted, as Roy Porter demonstrated in his *The Enlightenment* [133], that in England and Scotland the movement enjoined a repudiation of the logic of the religious conflicts and the accompanying intolerance that had ravaged the two countries in the era of the English civil war. The Enlightenment here meant religious toleration and the development of a vibrant public sphere, with coffee house discussions and a boom in periodical publications, as described by Jürgen Habermas [67]. However, on the continent the move was in the direction of absolute monarchies, and in the end the radical repudiation of absolutism provoked the French revolution of 1789. Koselleck notes how the critique of the eighteenth century provoked a crisis whose first major symptom was the French revolution [93].

In the nineteenth century this idea of political revolution was combined with a social agenda, above all by Marx, based on the idea that through an act of political rupture society could achieve its emancipation not only from oppression but also from subordination to contingency in the very broadest sense. This is what we call *emancipatory revolutionism*, and this was the project that in one way or another Lenin and Stalin sought to implement in Russia and, after the Second World War, in eastern Europe. Epochal thinking since the ancient world is characterised by a sense of the unfolding of time; but in the modern era, as we saw in the previous chapter, this became allied to a progressive understanding of social change. The new type of revolution shifted the axis of conflict to the class struggle within states, considered to be the motor of history, and thus the long twentieth century was characterised by a type of permanent internal cold war. In nineteenth-century Russia this cold war took increasingly sharp forms, and in the end took the very real form of civil war, and ushered in seven decades of communist rule.

The Russian revolution was the first large-scale attempt to implement Marxist revolutionary theory, the first attempt to build a society based on the rejection of western modernity while trying to fulfil it. This utopian project, as it is now called, displaced political discourse from pragmatic reason towards a political practice that generated closure and exclusivity. The pursuit of transcendent and universal (epochal) goals undermined appreciation of the particularism of the raw human material and national specificity of the country in which the revolutionaries had to work. In practice communism everywhere assumed national forms, but the tension between universalism (communism as an international movement) and particularism (the national vessel in which it was contained) did not disappear.

The Russian intelligentsia acted as the mediator between the ideas generated in western Europe and Russian society [126]. Already in the early eighteenth century, as Sergei Bulgakov put it in his contribution to the *Vekhi* collection, 'For good or evil, the fate of Petrine Russia was in the hands of the intelligentsia, however much it was persecuted and chased, and however much at that time the intelligentsia appeared weak and powerless. It is that eye cut through (*prorublennoe*) by Peter to Europe, through which the western spirit reaches us, at the same time both nourishing and poisonous' [23: *18*]. In other words, Peter's opening to the west was achieved not only by the physical creation of Petersburg, but also by the development of the intelligentsia as a class with concerns similar to intellectuals in the west. Russia's tragedy was that Peter fostered the creation of a western-type intelligentsia but failed to tie it to the development of a western-type bourgeoisie. This would have tempered some of the radicalism and utopianism of the isolated Russian intelligentsia. Hence there was a major difference between the western intellectuals and the Russian intelligentsia.

One of the peculiarities of Russian history is the contempt in which 'bourgeois' culture is held, and to a degree the west as a whole [34]. While Germany might have had a problem with its bourgeoisie, Russia's intelligentsia has historically proved an awkward class. The Russian revolutionary intelligentsia waged a struggle on two fronts: condemning the autocracy in Russia, but at the same time decrying western 'bourgeois' culture, with its obsession with individualism and private property. The condemnation of the bourgeoisie was not the preserve of the revolutionary intelligentsia but permeated all classes and strata of Russian society, from nationalists to anarchists. The upper classes viewed the bourgeoisie with their usual patrician disdain, while peasants and workers were fired by ideas of social justice and equality. The nascent Russian bourgeoisie had quite simply failed to become a hegemonic class before 1917 [12], although this had been developing rapidly in the late tsarist period. Hatred of the bourgeoisie characterised Russian development in the nineteenth century, and became the defining feature of the Russian revolution. Like the vision of class as a whole, the bourgeois category remained undefined and simply reflected a bundle of prejudices. It allowed others to define themselves as superior, whether from aristocratic heights, from the intellectual snobbery of the intelligentsia in the middle, or from the depths of proletarian suffering. François Furet, the historian of the French revolution, contemptuously dismisses such views, arguing that 'The bourgeoisie is a synonym for modern society' [51: 4], and, in extirpating the bourgeoisie, communism in Russia eradicated the fundamental elements that comprise a functioning system in contemporary conditions.

German society, too, had been permeated by contempt for liberalism and the bourgeoisie, and in many respects German and Russian critiques of modern bourgeois society have much in common. As early as 1903 the philosopher V. V. Rozanov, the author of *The Apocalypse of Our Times*, noted the similarities between Friedrich Nietzsche and Konstantin Leont'ev (1831–91), as two halves of the same comet, one of which had fallen in Germany and the other in Russia. Both condemned 'bourgeois' (*meshchanskuyu*) civilisation and warned against 'equality', 'justice' and 'peace', and both sang the praises of the elite and nobility of spirit. The conservative

'Byzantophile' (rather than Slavophile) Leont'ev warned against the 'cholera of democracy' and condemned 'accursed progress', stating 'we hate you, contemporary Europe!' and proclaimed that 'the Russian nation was especially not intended for freedom'. He was willing to contemplate socialism as long as it increased the power of the state. In short, Leont'ev graphically illustrates Alexander Yanov's assertion [195: 5] that there is an objective logic in the evolution of this strand of Slavophile (Byzantophile) Russian nationalism, from a protest against despotism to an apologia for it. Leont'ev was taken up in the late Soviet era by the 'Young Guard' romantic nationalists, who extolled him as the prophet of strong state power and the advocate of the application of military methods in the management of civil society.

There was a powerful contrary tendency that tried to 'normalise' Russia, in the sense that they repudiated not only the ideology of revolutionary socialism but also the political logic on which it was based, warning against the ethical consequences of trying to implement such a utopian project. This was reflected, as noted, in the *Vekhi* (*Landmarks*) collection of 1909, which brought together a remarkable group of thinkers, including the philosophers Nikolai Berdyaev and Semyon Frank, the economist and later theologian Sergei Bulgakov, and the political theorist Peter Struve. The critique of revolutionary socialism in the *Vekhi* collection was continued in a sequel, *Iz glubiny* (*From the Depths*), compiled in 1918 [76]. Less than a year after the October revolution the authors unerringly identified the weaknesses of the ideology that had come to power. Both volumes sought to demonstrate the lack of viability of the communist project in its economic and ethical aspects, and suggested an alternative based on a distinctive combination of humanistic Christian values and traditional civic virtues, a type of liberalism with a Russian face. The authors condemned the sectarian and narrow adoption by Russian intellectuals of the western Enlightenment tradition in its nineteenth-century positivist, atheistic and materialistic guise, which later combined to give the world 'scientific socialism' [182]. The *Vekhi* authors ultimately sought to preserve independent civic associations and associative life for Russia. In the half-century since the great reforms of the 1860s the country had seen a gradual structuration of urban society along modern lines and the beginnings of a more hegemonic type of relationship between the state and society; that is, one not based pre-eminently on coercion, although that is not to say that there were not profound contradictions in the social order.

The *Vekhi* tradition was resumed in 1974 in a third remarkable volume entitled *Iz-pod glyb* (*From Under the Rubble*), which included articles by Alexander Solzhenitsyn, Igor Shafarevich and Mikhail Agursky. The contributors to the new volume insisted that contemporary Russia could only be understood in the light of the intellectual traditions in Russian thought that had opposed the old revolutionary intelligentsia, and that this tradition had to be resumed. As with their predecessors, they once again stressed the need for a moral revolution and vigorously rejected the revolutionary view that a world turned upside down would lead to universal happiness [163]. This volume, like its predecessors, stressed Russia's unique path based on traditional spiritual values, but, while the *Vekhi* tradition explored the features of Russian exceptionalism, it also suggested a method to achieve the reconciliation of universal processes with Russia's specific traditions.

One of the notable aspects of the *Vekhi* tradition is its rejection of the prevalent anti-bourgeois sentiments. They insisted that workers and the bourgeoisie morally were one and the same, since both were motivated by the same material stimuli and shared universal human characteristics: in aspirations, workers were just as bourgeois as the bourgeoisie. Alexander Izgoyev argued in his contribution to *Iz glubiny* that the most creative elements in western socialism were precisely its bourgeois aspects, such as the right to private property, independent trade unions and the patriotic sentiments of the workers. They condemned class politics and warned that the ascription of law as 'bourgeois' and the condemnation of abstract categories like 'the bourgeoisie' as 'enemies of the people' would encompass ever wider groups including genuine traders, intellectuals and small farmers, and ultimately, we may add, anyone who happened to be inconvenient to the regime at the time. Thus, while stressing a distinctive Russian spiritual culture, these thinkers welcomed the advent of liberal and civic rights. While the call of revolution was at its loudest in Russia, from the first there was an opposed tradition that warned against its political and ethical consequences.

2 Bolshevism and its Critics

The political prerogatives of the autocracy increasingly came into conflict with the modernising impulse of the Russian state and economic and social developments. There was a fundamental incompatibility between imperial ambitions and the existing structure of power in a world undergoing a technological transformation. Russian defeats in the Russo-Japanese war of 1904–5 confirmed the lessons of the Crimean War (1854–6) a half-century earlier: substantial reforms were required for the Russian state to meet the heavy demands of modern warfare. The Japanese were themselves a good example of how this grafting could be achieved. Military reform in Russia would have been completed by 1916, and this in part set the German timetable for war in 1914. The revolution of 1905 resulted in due course in the establishment of a constitutional monarchy (although skewed towards the monarchy), but Russia ultimately failed to assimilate technological modernisation and economic change to a conservative social and political framework, and the whole edifice collapsed under the strain of war in February 1917. After only eight months of precarious rule, the Provisional Government in turn was overthrown by the Bolsheviks in October 1917, and a new era in Russian history began – the communist experiment that was to last seventy-four years.

Marxism and Bolshevism

Three elements came together to shape communism in Russia: *historicism*, the belief that, since the triumph of socialism was inevitable, history itself contained the answers to the necessary forms of socialist political organisation; *determinism*, the assumption that economic development would allow the emergence of the desired end condition; and *voluntarism*, the active involvement of agency in the historical process, whatever the actual level of socio-economic development. These three aspects were in permanent tension and shaped debates before 1917 and thereafter moulded the outcome of the Bolshevik seizure of power. The belief in the socialist end accompanied by the active remoulding of social and political relations encouraged authoritarian relations between the state and society. Law and the individual were subordinated to the end; and the means was justified on the grounds of historical determinism.

The movement that honoured Marx's name in its title impoverished his thinking in practice. Marx's shortcomings as a political scientist are well known: by denouncing 'bourgeois' constitutionalism and law, he provided no institutional defence of the individual against state power; but his view of positive freedom retains the power to inspire. For him freedom was not that of the 'negative' sort (to use Isaiah Berlin's terminology) that liberals espouse, freedom from external constraint for people to become what they wish to be, but a positive programme for people to become what they are. This is the freedom to realise the human essence, what Marx called 'species being'; freedom is thus something to be fulfilled a priori according to a formula revealed by Marx 'for others' rather than something to be attained in an ad hoc manner for oneself [187].

Marx's long-time collaborator, Engels, however, reduced this idea to a much simplified version of historical determinism in which humans were not much more than the sum of the circumstances in which they found themselves. Of the notion of human essence, and the achievement of freedom through its realisation, little remained. Instead, freedom came to be defined as liberation from the 'anarchy' of the market by the imposition of conscious control. The greater the collective control over the common affairs of humanity, the greater the freedom for its members, although individually they will have been reduced to little more than cogs in the machine. For Engels it was the rational organisation of the modern factory that provided a model for the organisation of the entire economy, a view taken up by Lenin in 1918 in the guise of the German war economy. Engels gave Marx's thinking a 'necessitarian' twist: that is, that history followed a necessary and rational logic. Lenin took up this theme, arguing that revolution was inevitable, but gave it yet another turn: revolution might be inevitable, but history had to be helped on its way and consciously shaped.

Lenin's philosophy of history combined necessitarianism (determinism) and voluntarism, and this shaped the fate of the socialist movement in Russia. The Russian Social Democratic Labour Party (RSDLP) was founded in Minsk in 1898, but from the first it was divided over tactics in relation to the tsarist authorities and over strategies of economic development. Lenin attacked the argument of the Economists and Legal Marxists that the working class should restrict its struggles to economic rather than political issues while waiting for the economy to develop. The newspaper *Iskra* (*The Spark*), founded by Lenin, Julius Martov, Plekhanov and others in 1900, helped bridge the gap between the workers and the intelligentsia, but served to divide the Social Democratic movement. In 1902 Lenin published his polemical pamphlet *What is to be Done?*, which according to the traditional interpretation outlined his concept of a tightly knit organisation of dedicated revolutionaries that would lead the class struggle of the proletariat. Somewhat reminiscent of Auguste Blanqui's principle of the small number, Lenin wrote 'Give us a revolutionary organisation and we will turn Russia upside down'. The Leninist inflexion of Russian revolutionary socialism is usually interpreted as the assimilation of Marxism to Russian traditions, but, as we shall see, this view has been criticised.

Lenin modified Marx's thinking about revolutionary organisation, which had stressed that the liberation of the working class would be achieved by the working class itself: it would first become a class 'in itself', and then a class 'for itself'. Marx never explained how this could be done, and Lenin provided the answer. The heart of Leninism is a theory of the role of the revolutionary party. Lenin was dismissive of the idea that the revolution would develop spontaneously in some sort of organic and spontaneous relationship with the working class. Instead he adopted an activist approach whereby the party should be prepared, in the right circumstances, actively to intervene in the revolutionary process. The corollary of this was an instrumental approach within the labour movement itself. Lenin argued that the working class on its own could only develop a trade union consciousness (i.e., would only concern itself with wages, conditions and so on, and not with changing the fundamental exploitative structure of society) and hence needed to be guided from outside by the revolutionary party. Lenin's notion of 'trade union consciousness' was akin to Marx's 'false consciousness', whereby workers suffer the 'blinding' effects of alienation. The critical role of the intelligentsia in devising the revolutionary programme and leading the masses was clearly reminiscent of the Populists, and indeed Lenin drew many of his ideas, including some of his thoughts on party organisation, from them.

Equally, the charge that Lenin 'Russified' Marxism has been questioned, since his arguments on party organisation and its broader role were firmly within the mainstream of Second International thinking and were espoused in a very similar way by Karl Kautsky at the head of the German Social Democratic Party (SDP), the largest socialist party of the time and the recognised leader of the movement. Kautsky was also one of the leading theoreticians of orthodox Marxism, and profoundly influenced Lenin's thinking. Kautsky was one of the co-authors (together with August Bebel and Eduard Bernstein) of the Erfurt Programme of the SDP in 1891, which predicted the imminent end of capitalism. The Programme called for the public ownership of the means of production, but advocated non-revolutionary legal forms of socialist struggle to improve workers' lives while waiting for capitalism to expire.

Lars Lih claims that Lenin's fundamental argument in *What is to be Done?* – about revolutionary consciousness being brought from the outside to a working class that, left to its own devices, would achieve no more than a reformist 'trade union consciousness' – has been fundamentally misunderstood [105]. Instead, according to Lih, Lenin was doing no more than what Kautsky had outlined in his discussion of the Erfurt Programme – to create a modern social democratic party of the west European type in which socialism and the labour movement combine. Although Lih convincingly argues that Lenin was dismissive of the Blanquist voluntarism associated with Pëtr Tkachev, the idea that a small group on its own could seize power and transform society, he concedes that Lenin consistently misrepresented the arguments of his opponents to discredit them. Lenin wrote the tract not out of a sense of crisis but in an attempt to seize the opportunities, above all a growing workers' movement, and he was impatient of those who stood in his way.

Certainly, Lenin was a man of his time and his arguments need to be understood in the context of the polemical debates of the period, but even a cursory reading of *What is to be Done?* reveals a contemptuous and dismissive attitude to the workers as the subject of their own history, and thus relied on the revolutionary intelligentsia to act as the vanguard of the proletariat. This was a feature of Lenin's thinking that was criticised by his fellow Bolshevik Alexander Bogdanov, who believed in the creative potential of the working class and after the revolution tried to put his ideas into practice through the *Proletkult* (proletarian culture) movement until suppressed by Lenin in 1920. Although Lenin was undoubtedly influenced by Kautsky, it would be an exaggeration to see him as a consistent Erfurtian (that is, ready to give up revolutionary forms of struggle). Lenin indeed drew his inspiration from veterans of the Russian revolutionary movement such as Plekhanov, who had argued for engagement with existing political structures rather than an obsession with social revolution. He was also influenced by Pavel Akselrod, who in 1889 had argued that the concerns of the workers had to be buttressed by the social goals of the intelligentsia. But ultimately the core of Leninism is the readiness to engage in revolutionary activity.

Lenin's approach was single-minded, and, while not lacking flexibility, it marginalised coalition-building and voluntary unity. At the second congress of the RSDLP in 1903 in London a division took place over Lenin's wording in the party programme of 'personal participation' for members, whereas Martov defended a broad definition of party membership, arguing for the formulation 'personal support'. The actual vote on the party statutes was lost by Lenin, but his group achieved a majority of two in the elections to the editorial board of *Iskra* and hence adopted the name Bolsheviks ('the majority') while Martov's group was condemned to labour under the moniker of 'the minority' (Mensheviks). Lenin, while personally modest, had an absolutely immodest political persona. He was intolerant of critics of his views, tending to anathematise them rather than dealing logically with points of disagreement. Intellectual differences thus had a tendency to be elevated very quickly into points of principle that brooked no compromise. Lenin's views became identified with the only correct path, and his opponents were not just mistaken but rendered enemies of the workers' revolution. In the end the Mensheviks and all other critics of Bolshevism became victims of this implacable logic.

While it is poor philosophy to argue that Marx begat Lenin and Lenin begat Stalin, since this discounts other possibilities, certain lines of development can be traced. In Lenin's theory, as Leon Trotsky (not yet a Bolshevik) prophetically pointed out in 1904, there was the danger of the party substituting for the working class, and the process would not stop there: 'The party is replaced by the organisation of the party, the organisation by the Central Committee, and finally the Central Committee by the dictator' [177]. The charge could equally have been laid against the German party, although Lenin took what became known as the theory of substitutionism to greater lengths.

The argument that Bolshevism is a heavily Russified version of Marxism has been challenged, and instead recent scholarship suggests that western Marxism and Russian Bolshevism had more in common than is usually allowed. Van Ree [184] questions a number of traditional assumptions. First, Marx was rather more open to the possibility of the revolution taking place not in a mature industrial society, where the industrial proletariat was in a majority, but in a relatively underdeveloped peasant society, and thus Lenin was exploiting an aspect of Marx's thinking that suggested the possibility of alliances with other classes. The founding fathers of what became known as 'scientific communism', Marx and Engels, were never fixated by the theory of stages in the revolutionary process. In his response to the Populist Vera Zasulich's letter of 16 February 1881 asking whether the peasant commune could be used as the basis for socialism or whether it was destined to perish, Marx on 8 March left open the possibility that Russia could skip stages, and thus fully-fledged industrial capitalism did not necessarily have to have developed in Russia before it could consider revolution.

Second, the notion of the revolutionary vanguard substituting for the weak proletariat, and thus justifying the dictatorship of a minority, is not unique to Russia. The Jacobin Blanquist tradition, after all, was devised not in Russia but in western Europe, and thus Leninism was in good company, although Marx had indeed been highly critical of Blanquist vanguardism. Third, the argument that the alleged inversion of the historical process, whereby industrialisation came first and only then the socialist revolution, forced the Bolsheviks to abandon the emancipatory goals of socialism while the economic foundations of the new society were built is contested. State-sponsored modernisation was not alien to Marx's thinking, and the alleged need to suppress political pluralism within the revolution as a result does not logically follow.

Fourth, the minority nature of the leadership and revolutionary modernisation from above accentuated the role of the bureaucracy and postponed the abolition of the state. Marx had always been vague about what he meant by 'the dictatorship of the proletariat', and above all what 'dictatorship' was to mean: would it be simply the dominance of the proletariat over other classes, or would it take a directly political form? David Lovell [107], who has examined Marx's 'responsibility' for Bolshevik authoritarianism, is inclined to the latter view, noting that Marx on many occasions called for revolutionary terrorism to suppress the resistance of the property-owning classes. Lenin's unwavering view that only the Bolsheviks represented the true interests of the proletariat, combined with Marx's readiness to condone forceful measures against the bourgeoisie and its acolytes, at the minimum prepared the conditions for repressive measures.

Fifth, the failure of the revolution to spread and the isolation of the revolution in Russia led Stalin to claim that socialism could be built in a single country. The idea of socialism in one country, according to van Ree, had a long pedigree in SDP thinking, and thus, as with the party, Stalin drew on Kautsky's ideas. And, finally, in the end the revolution became 'nationalised', whereby state patriotism ultimately became a form of Russian nationalism. As van Ree notes, however, even when in *The Communist Manifesto* Marx and Engels had famously proclaimed that 'The workers have no fatherland', this was immediately followed by a passage in which they envisaged that workers in the first instance would have to constitute themselves as the nation, although in due course communism would become universal. The writings of Marx and Engels are permeated by geopolitical thinking that pitched the Germanic nations against Slavic autocracy.

In sum, although clearly the socialist revolution took on a national colouring in Russia as it adapted to local conditions, Leninism and Stalinism were not such a drastic revision of Marxism as suggested by much traditional commentary. There is a constant interaction between the core and operating ideology, with both being interpreted in response to the exigencies of the political situation. This had been a feature of Marx's thinking in the first place, and it is this ontological instability at the heart of Marxism that prevents any easy argument that the original purity of the ideology was in some way debased by its exposure to Russian conditions. Communism in Russia was precisely that: the evolution of an idea in interaction with context and practice.

The 'freest country in the world'

The problem still remained of how to make the revolution in Russia. The breakdown in the finances of the autocracy was one of the main factors that led to its overthrow. A system of income tax had been introduced in summer 1916, but none had been collected by the time of the February revolution. Nicholas II was overthrown by what was in effect a palace coup in February 1917. The Provisional Government, led in its final period by Alexander Kerensky, replaced imperial rule, but itself lasted a mere eight months. This period is known in Marxist terminology as 'bourgeois democratic'; but, as even Lenin acknowledged, it made Russia the freest country in the world. The monarchy was overthrown, but after only eight months of 'bourgeois democracy' under the Provisional Government the Bolsheviks seized power in October 1917. The Bolsheviks were able to exploit the revolutionary potential of the peasantry, millions of whom had been drafted into the army, to make a socialist revolution. A fateful gulf between the self-proclaimed revolutionary vanguard and the great mass of the population was present from the very beginning. The failure of the democratic experiment in 1917 was not something determined by Russian political culture but was precipitated by a combination of domestic and external factors, primarily the war.

The Provisional Government granted a whole range of liberal freedoms, but, as often noted, freedom in Russia has always had anarchic connotations, and Russia under the Provisional Government was simply *too* democratic, granting too many freedoms before a robust constitutional framework of order guaranteeing the rule of law and the self-restraint of civil society could become routinised in constitutionalism, custom and tradition. The mass democracy lacked the mediating and constraining institutions of representative democracy. Freedom (*svoboda*), as so often in Russian history, became arbitrariness and licence (*proizvol*). The political system became overloaded and lacked a way of integrating and structuring the excessive demands from society. In other words, institutional development lagged behind popular aspirations. There were no credible democratic elites or representative institutions to filter the mass demands for land and social justice, and it failed to build a mass base of parties and parliament to legitimate itself. The middle class lacked time to create a political framework for civil society, building on the proto-hegemonic developments discussed above. February 1917 was a revolution without revolutionaries, lacking ruthlessness to defend its original aspirations to create a liberal democratic order. Its flexibility too often looked like weakness, and its readiness to embrace the agenda of its revolutionary protagonists deprived it of a natural base of its own.

The definition of democracy in the Russian popular and socialist tradition did not focus on a set of institutions that would defend a set of civic and human rights while ensuring limited government; instead, 'democracy' was equated with the people. This was a social rather than an institutional definition of democracy and was the essence of the broader Russian revolution. The power of the people was counterposed not to dictatorship but to the privileged and ruling classes; and in 1917 the 'democratic camp' encompassed the whole of the working masses and the revolutionary democracy [89]. In that sense, the Bolsheviks were a 'democratic' party, in that they based their rule on the rhetoric of popular power; but, in the institutional sense of democracy being a system of accountable authority where governments are changed through popular ballots, the communist system was the antithesis of democracy. The 'democracy' of 1917 tended to exclude the bourgeoisie, and thus a priori the basis for a liberal polity was undermined and instead workers and peasants became 'the people', although the revolutionary intelligentsia was also included [169: *20*].

From the outset the political revolution of February 1917, which reflected at first the deepest aspirations of the Russian revolution, had the potential to take a maximal turn. The system of 'dual power' inaugurated in February meant that the government had to share power with the resurgent soviets (councils), first created during the 1905 revolution, which were being formed throughout the country. The famous Order Number One of 1 March of the Petrograd Soviet called for the election of committees in all military units and contributed massively to the disintegration of the Russian army. The order deprived the government of control over troop dispositions. The soviets in 1917 were organised loosely, but soon their executive committees, composed of socialist politicians and intellectuals, dominated the rank-and-file delegates in the plenums. Robert Michels' 'iron law of oligarchy' was once again at work.

The Provisional Government failed to find a mass or a political base of support. Russia had been in expectation of a revolution for over 100 years, but when it finally took place it did so at a time of war and social dislocation, which undermined its constitutional aspirations. The middle class was weak and lacked an adequate form of political representation. As for a political base, the parties that supported the Provisional Government were weakened by association with its failed policies. Morgan Philips Price, an astute observer reporting for the *Manchester Guardian*, noted in August 1917 that the crisis of the revolution stemmed from one elementary fact: 'material exhaustion resulting from the attempt to carry on a foreign war and an internal revolution at the same time' [134: 52]. It was war that had destroyed the autocracy, and it would consume the Provisional Government as well; as John Bright had remarked, 'war destroys the Government that makes it'. Price went on to note that the revolution faced an almost impossible task. Unable to turn to reconstruction in a time of war, 'It tries to rebuild on the ruins of the old, but its neighbours in Western Europe persist in making it continue to destroy and thereby sap all its remaining strength. The machine of the old Russian State has collapsed, but nothing has come in its place because the whole attention of the country has still to be turned on works of destruction' [134: 52].

The Bolsheviks stood for nationalisation of land and the proletarianisation of the peasantry, whereas the Socialist Revolutionaries hoped to draw on the rich potential of the peasants' communal traditions, freed at last from the lingering remnants of feudal oppression but not yet tainted by western commercialism. For them the peasant was to be neither proprietor, as desired by the Constitutional Democrats (Kadets), nor wage slave, as anticipated by the Marxists, but a free member of a collective social unit, the peasant commune. All except the Kadets and other 'bourgeois' parties, who anticipated that the Russian *muzhik* could be transformed into the yeoman farmer of the English or French type, sought to abolish landlordism and the right of private property. The peasant commune did indeed enjoy great vitality at this time, as Sorokin had noted. Price describes a meeting in Samara *guberniya* in September 1917:

> Next day there was a meeting of the rural commune. Outside the common barn, in the middle of the village street, the peasants had gathered. The heads of families and every working hand including sons, if

there were any now, were present. I also saw quite a number of women... Here in fact was the most elementary unit of Russian rural society. It has existed for centuries and is rooted deep in the Middle Ages. It is essentially democratic, for women have equal rights with men. The revolution when it came had only to make use of this institution. [134: *60*]

The Bolshevik revolution

In 1917 the major division ultimately was not between socialism and liberalism but within socialism itself, between revolutionary and evolutionary socialism, a break that was then projected onto the world stage. The Bolshevik revolution represented a revolution within the revolution, striking against the democratic socialists as much as against a still tenuous bourgeois order. It was a pre-emptive blow against bourgeois development rather than the overthrow of a mature system that had reached the limits of its developmental potential. On returning to Russia in April (courtesy of the Germans in a sealed railway carriage, delivered to the Finland Station), to the astonishment even of his fellow Bolsheviks, Lenin in his 'April Theses' insisted that the transition should continue from the first stage of the revolution, where the bourgeoisie had taken power in a political overturn in the absence of a sufficiently revolutionary proletariat, to the second stage in which a social revolution would transfer power to the working people (or their representatives), who by now would have grown in consciousness. This was a variation of Trotsky's idea of the 'permanent revolution', in which the 'bourgeois–democratic' revolution should uninterruptedly grow into a workers' revolution. The idea that 'imperialism broke at its weakest link' in 1917 was not one that Lenin advanced at the time, and instead was ascribed to him by Stalin later. Nevertheless, following his arrival back in Russia Lenin obsessively watched for signs of the international revolution and believed that the European social revolution would have to come to Russia's assistance if socialism were to be built. In the meantime, the Bolsheviks would have to hang on to power at any cost.

The Bolsheviks seized power on 25 October 1917 (7 November in the new-style calendar, thirteen days ahead of the old), and thus put an end to Russia's first democratic 'transition'. Kerensky's government fell to the Bolshevik insurgents, Price argued, because 'it had no supporters in the country. The bourgeois parties and

the generals at the Staff disliked it because it would not establish
a military dictatorship. The revolutionary democracy lost faith in
it because after eight months it had neither given land to the peasants nor established State control of industries nor advanced the
cause of the Russian peace programme. Instead it brought off the
July advance [the catastrophic offensive forced on Russia to relieve
pressure on the western front] without any guarantee that the
Allies had even agreed to reconsider war aims' [134: *88*].

There were a number of revolutions in 1917, while even within
the Bolshevik party there were different visions of the conduct of
politics: Bolsheviks, Leninists and proto-Stalinists. The October
revolution was effectively six revolutions rolled into one:

1. The mass social revolution, in which peasants sought land, soldiers (peasants in another guise) struggled for peace, and workers for greater recognition in the labour process.
2. The democratic revolution, expressing aspirations for the development of political accountability and popular representation,
   although not necessarily in classic liberal democratic forms.
3. The liberal revolution, in which the nascent bourgeoisie repudiated the absolutist claims of divine rule by the monarchy and
   fought to apply what they considered to be more enlightened
   forms of constitutional government and secure property rights.
4. The national revolution, which confirmed the independence
   of Poland and Finland, and saw the rapid fragmentation of
   the Russian empire. The Provisional Government's failure
   to respond to the national aspirations of Ukraine, the South
   Caucasian and the Central Asian republics was one of the reasons for its downfall.
5. The revolution of internationalism. The Russian revolution
   reflected a trend of thought, exemplified by Marx, which
   suggested that the old-style nation state was redundant and, as
   capitalism became a global system, so social orders would gradually lose their national characteristics. From this perspective
   the revolution could just as easily have taken place in Berlin or
   Paris; it just happened to start in what Lenin reputedly called
   'the weakest link in the imperialist chain', in St Petersburg and
   Moscow, but would according to him inevitably spread.
6. The revolution within the revolution: as the most extreme wing
   of the Russian revolution, the Bolsheviks usurped the agenda of

the moderate socialists, mobilising workers and revolutionary idealists (such as the anarchists) to establish their own political dictatorship. The Bolsheviks were the most ruthless and effective advocates of the radical emancipation of the people in the name of a new set of social ideals. This radical agenda stemmed from the combination of Enlightenment and emancipatory revolutionism, as reworked by Marx.

The interrelationship and tension between these six levels of revolution are what make the October revolution so perennially fascinating, but these contradictions were ultimately resolved not by debate but by war and terror.

The Bolshevik seizure of power was followed by the Decree on Land of 26 October 1917 granting peasants full use of the land, and a decree declaring Russia's withdrawal from the First World War. This was accompanied by an assault on big business ('the Red Guard attack on capital'), as well as against the free press. The secret police, the Emergency Commission for the Struggle Against Counter-Revolution, abbreviated to Cheka, was established on 2 December 1917, the forerunner of many Soviet repressive agencies. Its first head was Felix Dzerzhinsky, born into the minor Polish gentry, who had planned to become a priest before turning into a fanatical proselyte in the new faith of socialism. He was a genuine believer that violence was necessary to defend the revolution, but was not personally a sadist – he left that work to his subordinates Eiduk, Peters and Atarbekov, not one of whom, it is often pointed out, was an ethnic Russian.

At first the Bolsheviks had no clear idea of the form that the new state would take. It was to be revolutionary, but not necessarily 'soviet'. This was revealed by the plans not to abolish but to re-elect the Moscow City Duma, a body that had organised opposition to the Bolshevik seizure of power in the city. Indeed, resistance to the Bolshevik usurpation of the ideals of the Russian revolution was at its strongest in Moscow, where hegemonic strategies had sunk their deepest roots, and was defeated only by echelons of Kronstadt sailors and Latvian riflemen sent from Petrograd. Even after the Bolshevik victory the idea of dual power remained influential. There appears to have been a limited view of the soviets as exercising a type of political '*kontrol*' (that is, supervision) over the work of the old city administration. Lenin's *State and Revolution* had still not been published (it only saw the light of day in 1918), but when written in 1917 its talk of smashing the old state apparatus and bringing the people into government reflected the utopian strain in Bolshevism, but even in this text the need for central control was stressed [131].

Bolshevism in Leninist form represented a radical repudiation of classical representative democracy. The development of the institutions of commune democracy, exercised formally by soviets of people's deputies, was based on a system of delegation and sectoral representation. Accountability was to be exercised directly by electors in their ability to recall their delegates from soviets. In *The Civil War in France* Marx had argued that in this way the social powers alienated to the state were brought back to society. Lenin took up this theme in his *The State and Revolution* as he sought to find a way to structure the political institutions of an emancipated society. Commune democracy failed to make allowance for opposition *within* the revolution, while of course suppressing opposition *to* the revolution, and thus utopian visions soon gave way to dystopian realities. The structure of authority relations that emerged was persistently archaic, with the communist party acting as the new collective prince, to use Gramsci's term. Republican ideals of an active and responsible citizenship failed to materialise and instead a new form of neo-monarchical patrimonial power was consolidated.

This phase rapidly gave way to 'soviet' power (that is, not the power of actual soviets, but of the Bolshevik party ruling in their name) when the Bolsheviks discovered that the soviets were an excellent instrument both to destroy the old institutions of central and local government and to administer society while retaining power in their own hands. Lenin liked to remind people that the Bolsheviks were 'not anarchists', and his language was permeated with the language of 'dictatorship' and 'iron discipline'; from the first days in power he showed no compunction about using mass arrests, terror and summary executions. These were not measures forced upon the Bolsheviks but were part of their Leninist make-up, and emerged out of the logic of the situation where a minority seizes and holds on to power against all the odds.

Even within the Bolshevik movement there was resistance to the Leninist formulation of communist power. The Bolshevik party had grown from a small group of about 25,000 in February 1917 to something around 300,000 in October, and the problem of managing this mass, which grew rapidly once the Bolsheviks became the ruling party, was achieved through various purges and discipline campaigns. Within the leadership the first major debate was over the organisation of Soviet power. The creation of an exclusively Bolshevik government in the form of the Council of People's Commissars (Sovnarkom) headed by Lenin on 25 October shocked those who had believed that power would be transferred to the soviets. The creation of Sovnarkom took power away from the Central Executive Committee (VTsIK) of the soviets, in whose name the revolution had been made, and power was transferred to a body responsible to no-one but the Bolshevik party itself. Moderates within the Bolshevik party objected to Lenin's coup, arguing that the manner of seizing power meant that the only way the Bolsheviks could stay on top was through civil war.

The coalitionists in the party called for the broadening of the government to include all parties represented in the soviets. A group including Lev Kamenev, Grigorii Zinoviev and Alexei Rykov insisted on the formation of a coalition government with some of the anti-war moderate socialists and envisaged a role for some organisations in addition to the soviets in the new system. They felt so strongly over the issue that they resigned from the new government, warning that Lenin's policies would lead to civil war. Lenin in November agreed to share power with the Left Socialist Revolutionaries (LSRs), which constituted itself as a separate party at that time. The arrangement lasted until March 1918, and following an alleged attempt at an uprising on 6 July the LSRs were severely persecuted. After a bitter struggle the coalitionists were defeated. This was the first instance of a major debate in a revolutionary party in power. Kamenev at the head of the Moscow Soviet would go on to become the most consistent critic of secret police power.

However, the Bolshevik moderates failed to take a consistent stand in defence of the long-awaited representative assembly. In the elections to the Constituent Assembly in November 1917 the Bolsheviks won in Petrograd and Moscow and gained almost a quarter of the total seats (147), but in the country as a whole the SRs (still a single group) gained a large majority (410 delegates). It is difficult to gauge how different the results might have been if the elections had been held a month later after the formal split of the SRs and when the Bolshevik land decree had become better known. The Assembly met on 5 January 1918, only to be dissolved that same day. Bukharin read a declaration stating that the

Bolsheviks 'declare war without mercy against the bourgeois parliamentary republic'. Soviet Russia's experiment with constitutional governance ended before it had begun. Lenin claimed that soviet power and the dictatorship of the proletariat was a far higher form of democracy, but the shooting of workers demonstrating in favour of the Assembly, in Petrograd and elsewhere, revealed the fate of those who disagreed.

The Russian empire's failure to resolve the 'nationality' problem was one of the main reasons for its demise in 1917–18. The weakening of central state power accelerated the centrifugal tendencies in the empire as a whole. As in the post-communist period, there was a tendency for the country 'to split up into a number of areas, each running its own internal policy...' [134: *63*]. By the end of the Civil War Poland, Finland, Estonia, Latvia, Lithuania, Armenia, Azerbaijan, Georgia, Ukraine and Belorussia had achieved, for varying periods, independence. The independence of Poland and Finland went largely unopposed, whereas the creation of Ukrainian and Transcaucasian national states was precarious and was undermined as soon as the Bolsheviks won the Civil War of 1918–20. Earlier declarations in favour of 'the right of nations to self-determination', notably in Lenin's 1916 pamphlet of that name, were modified in January 1918 by Joseph Stalin, the people's commissar of nationalities, who asserted that it was a right not of the bourgeoisie, but of the working people of a given nation. National liberation was subordinated to the class struggle. Nevertheless, a number of Bolshevik leaders hailed from the Caucasus, including Stalin and Sergo Ordzhonikdze, and they knew that traditional state-building programmes would have to be complemented by local strategies if Bolshevik power were to be secured. In that region it was communist promises to secure the position of Islam, sharia law and self-government that allowed the Bolsheviks to triumph against the White armies led by General Anton Denikin.

Bolshevik experiments

Lenin's definition of communist power in Russia responded to changed circumstances, and in this Lenin showed himself to be a brilliant political leader. He constantly devised new variations of the operative ideology while claiming its commensurability with core principles. Instead of waging a revolutionary war, as advocated by the Left Communists who sought to take the war to the 'imperialists', Lenin through the treaty of Brest–Litovsk in March 1918 removed Soviet Russia from the Great War, allowing Germany to transfer forces to the western front. The Germans imposed crushing terms as Lenin gave up territory to buy time. The treaty did not mean the repudiation of socialist internationalism, but it did represent a shift to communist nationalism. This was a period in which various oppositional groupings *within* the revolution advanced alternative policies. The leading coalitionists had resigned, and the Left Communists not only urged Lenin to wage a revolutionary war against Germany in the name of the internationalist principles of October, but also called on the party to trust the workers to manage their own affairs.

In the 'breathing space' that followed Lenin developed a strategy for Russia's development based on what he called *state capitalism*. Lenin sought to emulate the successes of the German war economy based on gigantic cartels, but without the bourgeois political infrastructure of law and parliament. Lenin negotiated with selected capitalists to form trusts through which he hoped that the enormous potential of modern industrial organisation could serve the socialist state. The compromise was to be with capitalism, not the bourgeoisie or with bourgeois democracy. The state capitalist period of April–May 1918 was accompanied by the struggle to restore labour discipline and raise labour productivity in the factories, complemented by enthusiasm for Frederick Taylor's time and motion studies on production lines. Indeed, Soviet power became the epitome of a Fordist model of industrial society, and it remained stuck with this approach long after it had been modified in the west. There was already in Lenin a strongly authoritarian attitude that spilled over to his view of the working class, exacerbated by the perceived developmental needs of society. In his *The Immediate Tasks of Soviet Power* of April 1918 Lenin asserted that 'The Russian is a bad worker compared to the workers of the advanced nations'; therefore the government must 'teach the people how to work', and therefore they must '*unquestioningly obey the single will* of the leaders of labour' (italics in original). Factory committees were subordinated to the Bolshevik trade union structure as the party sought to weaken syndicalist tendencies. The 'state capitalism' experiment revealed Lenin's ruthless pragmatism (as the peace of

Brest–Litovsk had done earlier) as the emancipatory goals of the mass revolution came into contradiction with the developmental goals of the regime. Lenin was devising the operative ideology as he went along, and he did so with considerable flexibility. Lenin's model of socialism appeared to be that of the German war economy without capitalists, a state capitalism where the state fulfilled the role of capitalists.

This was also the period when movements *against* the revolution began to mobilise, precipitating the Civil War in May 1918. Just as it would be simplistic to see the October revolution solely as a struggle of Bolshevik revolutionaries against counter-revolutionaries, rather than equally a struggle for the fate of the socialist revolution itself, so, too, the Civil War was far more complex than 'Whites' versus 'Reds'. The 'Whites' included some of the moderate socialists defeated in October 1917, among them a large part of the old Socialist Revolutionary party. Even the extent of Bolshevik support in the cities must be rethought, since right from the beginning there was a strong current of autonomous worker activity (for example, the Menshevik-inspired worker plenipotentiary movement of March–July 1918), which was defeated by Bolshevik coercion. Bolsheviks used extreme violence from the outset, fighting 'civil wars' against worker autonomy in the rear, against most of the peasantry, various national movements when their support was no longer required, some limited and half-hearted foreign intervention, and the Whites [25]. There was a multiplicity of 'civil wars', as opposed to a single red–white Civil War, as well as a number of foreign interventions, notably the British in the north. In fear of the advance of Czechoslovak forces, the royal family were shot on 17 July 1918 and the bodies of tsar Nicholas II, his wife Alexandra, their five children and their servants were doused with sulphuric acid and burnt. But it was not violence alone that sustained the Bolsheviks in power. With Admiral Kolchak's coup in late 1918 the plane of the Civil War tilted away from a struggle between Jacobin extremism and terror against a moderate socialist alternative towards a struggle between outright reactionaries fired by Russian messianic nationalism and Bolshevik 'progressivism', however distorted this was in practice.

The Civil War was a logical consequence of Bolshevik strategy: their seizure of power was an act of war against the 'exploiting classes' and 'imperialism'. During the Civil War fourteen countries intervened, but in most respects it was a real civil war. The Bolsheviks soon reconciled themselves to the use of former tsarist officers, known as 'military specialists' (*spetsy*), thousands of whom were drafted to provide military expertise as commanders under the supervision of Bolshevik commissars. The war was fought by the Bolsheviks largely as a traditional war, with centralisation and military discipline. A regular army was established on 23 February 1918, and under Leon Trotsky's ruthless but brilliant leadership the Bolsheviks were able to crush their enemies. Although the idea of a militia army lingered on into the 1920s, the long-standing Marxist prejudice against traditional standing armies was soon forgotten. The Bolsheviks enjoyed the advantage of holding the centre of the country and the railways radiating out of Moscow, but in the end the victory represented the triumph of the ideal of militant communism. Indeed, in 1920 Trotsky planned to militarise labour by redeploying the Red Army of 5 million to reconstruct the civilian economy. Trotsky sought to remodel society on the pattern of an army, and the Civil War reinforced the Bolshevik predisposition to a militaristic approach to social and political administration.

The Civil War was accompanied by War Communism, which lasted from mid-1918 to March 1921. The onset of the Civil War put an end to the state capitalist strategy, and in a pre-emptive move on 28 June 1918 the majority of Russian industry was nationalised. War Communism developed partially in response to the exigencies of fighting the war and the associated drive to gather authority and resources, but also reflected aspects of Bolshevik utopianism, such as the attempt to abolish private property over the means of production. Management of nationalised enterprises was concentrated in special economic councils (*sovnarkhozy*), rising in a pyramidal structure to the Supreme Economic Council (VSNKh, also known as *Vesenkha*) in Moscow. This system in effect represented a giant corporation divided into branches (*glavki*), holding the whole economic life of the country in its hands. To feed the cities and the Red Army a harsh system of grain expropriation was imposed on the peasantry. During the Civil War peasants often declared that they supported the Bolsheviks but not the communists, indicating approval for the decree on land but not the subsequent requisitioning policies or the communist policy favouring collectivised forms of agriculture. This was a period characterised by an unstable mix of ideological extremism and pragmatism, reflected in 1920, for example, by the abolition of money, which had become largely worthless anyway.

War Communism represented the necessary mobilisation of all resources in a time of war, but it also gave free rein to utopian projects for the total transformation of society. It reflected nine-teenth-century sociology, with its utopian belief that a direct leap could be made into socialism by administrative fiat. Immediate pressures of fighting a war interacted with ideological aspirations, with the war acting as the catalyst bringing out the most radical features of communist ideology. War Communism was a distinct-ive blend of revolutionary enthusiasm and pragmatism. Some war communist policies, such as the abolition of money, were not des-tined to outlive the Civil War, but others – notably economic and political centralisation, the abolition of private ownership in man-ufacturing and industry, and intense coercion – were to become a permanent part of communism in Russia. Workers' organisa-tions and trade unions lacked autonomy, with factory commit-tees restricted to agitprop functions as one-person management became the norm.

Bolshevik alternatives

The Bolshevik party became the kernel of the new political system, and by the end of the Civil War a uniform network of party committees had emerged under the central party Secretariat in Moscow. The principle of democratic centralism, with the subordination of lower to higher bodies, was established as earlier federal forms of organisation were eliminated. Mass participatory organisations were equally subordinated to the party, notably the trade unions and the Komsomol, established in 1919, and were to be imbued with the 'party spirit' (*partiinost'*), a fundamental principle of Soviet political life. The political system became increasingly centralised and bureaucratised.

These developments provoked a number of 'oppositions' within the Bolshevik party, renamed the Russian Communist Party (Bolsheviks) – the RCP (b) – in 1918. Four key issues were raised that were at the heart of the new polity: the role of the soviets; the rise of the bureaucracy; the problem of democracy within the party;

and relations with workers. On the first point, since the soviets contained non-Bolsheviks as well as peasants they were regarded with suspicion by the Bolshevik leadership. No effort was spared in applying 'administrative resources' to ensure that the right people were elected. The question remained, however, about how the party's 'leading role' could be reconciled with meaningful political functions for the soviets. The Democratic Centralists from late 1918 insisted that the relationship should be based on a division of labour: the party would provide ideological leadership, but the soviets should be integrated as institutions representing the working class. The first Soviet constitution of July 1918 was long on declarations of principle, but left the institutional arrangements for the actual organisation of power vague. The Democratic Centralists hoped to remedy the situation by revising the constitution to safeguard the rights of lower-level bodies from the encroachments of the centre. The Democratic Centralists demanded the introduction of the separation of powers within the regime itself, with greater autonomy for local soviets and lower-level party committees. They sought to institutionalise the revolution in the form of genuine soviet, rather than Bolshevik, power: that is, for a system based on genuine and independent authority for the soviets. The Eighth Party Congress in March 1919 agreed that the party should 'guide' the soviets, and not 'replace' them, though this formulation left the details vague and the problem of 'substitution' (*podmena*) remained to the end of communist rule. A novel form of dual power was established, which retained a revolutionary potential, one that was taken up later by Gorbachev when he revived the slogan 'all power to the soviets'. In the early years, however, the idea of the 'withering away of the state' was postponed to some indefinite future.

As for the bureaucracy, early communists believed that after the revolution public administration would be little more than a matter of book-keeping, and, as Bukharin and Evgenii Preobrazhensky put it in their *ABC of Communism* in 1919, 'There will be no need for special ministers of state, for police and prisons, for laws and decrees... The bureaucracy, the permanent officialdom, will disappear. The State will die out' [22: *118*]. In fact, quite the opposite occurred, and the problem of rampant bureaucracy was an obsession of the period and remained so to the end of the system. Its manifestations were legion: red tape, corruption and inefficiency. As the functions of the state expanded so the bureaucracy mushroomed.

Everywhere new committees and commissions were born, regulating in greater detail ever smaller segments of life. The numbers employed in bureaucratic administrations swelled to make up over a third of the labour force by 1921. The Bolsheviks were at a loss to comprehend the omnipotence of bureaucracy, all the more so since the theory of commune democracy held that bureaucracy would disappear in its entirety. Lenin insisted it was a social problem and reflected the lack of culture of Russia. Others insisted that it was a legacy of the tsarist regime that would be overcome in time. In fact, structural factors were at work: the attempt to run the whole life of the country from Moscow gave rise to the bureaucracy.

As the Civil War came to an end, two interrelated but separate debates challenged the structure of power as it had taken shape since the revolution. The 'party debate' focused on inner-party democracy and covered such issues as free speech within the party, the rights of party cells, the functions of the committees and the role of leadership. The polarisation of society between the *verkhi* (upper tier) and the *nizy* (the masses) had been internalised within the party, with the *verkhi* now represented by higher party officials, and the *nizy* by the party's rank and file. The 'trade union' debate focused on the role of worker organisations and plans to curb the power of the bureaucracy. The Workers' Opposition, led by Alexander Shlyapnikov and Alexandra Kollontai, insisted that more rights should be vested in the direct expression of workers' organisation. They called for a national congress of producers to take direct control of economic management. Kollontai criticised the bureaucratic regulation of all aspects of social existence, which included the attempt to instil *partiinost'* even in dog lovers' clubs. She urged that the initiative of the workers should be encouraged, and insisted that 'Wide publicity, freedom of opinion and discussion, the right to criticise within the party and among the members of the trade unions – such are the decisive steps that can put an end to the prevailing system of bureaucracy' [88]. It was at this time that Trotsky took War Communist practices to their logical conclusion and insisted that the unions should be incorporated into the economic apparatus. Lenin ultimately took a middle path: the unions should remain independent and act as educators of the working class rather than the organisers of production.

The 'party democracy' debate in the autumn of 1920 represented the last serious discussion about the need for some sort of public sphere within the party to avoid the bureaucratisation of the revolutionary government. It was rapidly, and possibly deliberately, eclipsed by the trade union debate launched by the Workers' Opposition. Although the latter raised some similar concerns to the party democratisers, above all the condemnation of bureaucracy, the addition of anti-intelligentsia (anti-specialist) themes and above all the claim that workers should run industry roused Lenin's hostility. While the party democratisers sought solutions at the level of political institutions, the Workers' Opposition reduced the question of political reform to the class dimension. As the Democratic Centralists had argued earlier, and reiterated in the party debate, the poor functioning of Soviet institutions derived more from problems (as we would now put it) of institutional design than from petty bourgeois elements worming their way in to advance their own careers. The portrayal of political issues as a matter of class played into the hands of the Leninists, and allowed the new regime to avoid a serious self-analysis of its nature. When the question was couched in class terms, Lenin was unequalled; it was to political problems that he had no solutions.

All of this demonstrates, according to Farber, that there were revolutionary alternatives [45] to dogmatic Bolshevism. This view rejects the cultural determinism that suggests that communism could have taken no other path than the one it did because of the character of Russia; and equally it rejects the ideological determinism, prevalent in totalitarian approaches, that suggests a straight line from Marxism to Stalinism. The Russian revolution, as Sorokin and countless other critics of tsarism demonstrated, was far broader than its particular Bolshevik manifestation. At the same time, as the party and trade union debates demonstrate, even though there were alternatives not only within the revolution but also in the Bolshevik party itself, the logic of Leninism inevitably tended towards the destruction of socialist diversity and pluralism, although the rationale of that logic adapted to circumstances. In 1917–18 Lenin justified exclusivity because of the logic of political struggle; in 1919–20 because of the logic of Civil War; and from 1920 because of the alleged social determinism prompted by the destruction of the working class and the economic imperative of implementing a strategy of economic development. Pirani, however, has shown that the Bolshevik assertion that the working class was destroyed by the end of the Civil War, which justified their own leadership, was much exaggerated; a conscious workers' movement remained with a sense of purpose and leadership [128]. Instead, old ideas of democratic socialism and social emancipation gave way to a bureaucratised and violent reality. Compulsion in external interactions and suppression within the party became mutually reinforcing, giving rise by the late 1920s to the ferociously coercive Stalinist system. This was not something visited upon the Bolsheviks from outside, as the opposition within the party pointed out, but was part of an intrinsic political process. The existence of alternatives only demonstrates the narrowness of the path actually taken.

With the Civil War effectively over by mid-1920, the momentum of Bolshevik ideological extremism nevertheless continued. This was manifested, for example, in the war against Poland in 1920, which sought to spread the revolution at the point of the Red Army's bayonets. The intensification of grain requisitioning, the militarisation of labour (a policy advocated by the commissar of war, Trotsky), and the closure of urban markets provoked peasant uprisings (notably in the Tambov region) and, most significantly, demands by workers at the Kronstadt naval base in the Gulf of Finland, formerly a bastion of revolutionary Bolshevism, in March 1921 for 'soviets without Bolsheviks' [7]. By early 1921 the system was in crisis. Peasant revolts in the countryside were compounded by urban unrest, and the revolt of workers and sailors at Kronstadt denounced the Bolshevik usurpation of the rights of the soviets. This represented a much greater threat to Bolshevik power than its outright opponents, and hence was dealt with accordingly.

With the regime under threat, Lenin at the Tenth Party Congress in March 1921 convinced his party to reverse its policies and make concessions to the peasantry. Compulsory grain deliveries were now replaced by a fixed tax in kind, allowing peasants to sell grain surpluses in a restored market. A limited degree of producer autonomy was introduced as part of the New Economic Policy (NEP). Lenin admitted that the attempt to continue the organisation of the economy by wartime means had been a mistake. War Communism, he insisted, had been necessitated by the war and dislocation but it was not a viable long-term policy. Lenin thus justified the necessity of War Communism and its repeal, a notable example of the flexibility inherent in the operating ideology. Economic concessions, however, were balanced by the intensification of war communist political processes. To secure the regime's flanks in this 'retreat', Lenin imposed draconian discipline within the party. The party debate was now stifled, and at the congress two decrees condemned the oppositional groupings and imposed a 'ban on factions', a 'temporary' measure which remained a cardinal principle of Soviet rule.

The Bolshevik dictatorship did not emerge full-blown in October 1917, and in its early years it was certainly far from the well-functioning system to which it aspired later, but in its relations with society and in internal party matters processes were set in train from the very first days that were later consolidated in the Stalinist bureaucratic machine. Although the Workers' Opposition complained about the restrictions on free speech within the party and tried to broaden the base of the regime by restoring elements of the mass revolution by granting broad economic rights to the trade unions, not only were they defeated but the very idea of opposition and legal debate within the Party was proscribed. The distinction between opposition to the revolution, by various forces outside the regime, and opposition within the system, by those seeking to explore alternative policy options, was extinguished, and the door opened to Stalin's monocratic rule.

The politics of utopia – a negative transcendence

By 1921 the enduring features of the Soviet order were in place. The RCP (b) ran according to the principles of 'democratic centralism': discussion was possible until a decision was taken by the ruling bodies, and thereafter undeviating implementation was incumbent upon all lower organs. The ban on factions, forbidding horizontal contacts between party cells, and other administrative measures reduced the scope for debate. The powers of the Politburo and the Secretariat at the head of the party were consolidated, with Stalin using his control of the latter to destroy opposition. With the creation of the Union of Soviet Socialist Republics (USSR) in December 1922, establishing the new state as a voluntary federation of what were originally four federal republics with the right of secession, and the adoption of the first Soviet constitution in January 1924, system-building was basically complete. There were even attempts to rein in the power of the secret police, beginning a long series of name changes that saw the Cheka become the

Main Political Administration (GPU), the United GPU (OGPU), the fearsome Peoples' Commissariat of Internal Affairs (NKVD), which conducted the great purges of the 1930s, and finally the Committee of State Security (KGB) in the post-Stalin era. Lenin died in January 1924, and by the end of the 1920s Stalin had established his personal rule. In 1929 he launched a murderous collectivisation campaign forcing the peasants into collective farms, and in the 1930s a series of purges destroyed the 'old Bolsheviks', the generation of leaders who had worked with Lenin. The great terror caught millions in its murderous web.

There had long been warnings about what might happen if abstract ideas for the betterment of humanity were applied to actual living societies. As the Russian anarchist and Marx's rival, Mikhail Bakunin, put it, describing the various intellectual schemes put forward by revolutionary socialists: 'Let him govern, and he will become the most unbearable tyrant, for scholarly pride is repulsive, offensive, and more oppressive than any other. To be the slaves of pedants – what a fate for mankind! Give them free rein, and they will start performing the same experiments on human society that for the sake of science they now perform on rabbits, cats, and dogs' [8: *134*]. Bakunin condemned the pretensions of those who claimed to understand the laws of history and, warming to his theme, he denounced intelligentsia schemes for the betterment of humanity: 'We will esteem scholars according to their merits, but for the salvation of their intellect and morality they must not be given any social privileges or accorded any other right than the common one of freedom to propagate their convictions, ideas and knowledge. Power should no more be given to them than to anyone else, for anyone who is invested with power by an invariable social law will inevitably become the oppressor and exploiter of society' [8: *134*]. These were prescient words, and the notion of the Bolshevik revolution as an 'experiment' is one to which we shall return.

The Civil War effectively crushed opposition to the revolution in Russia, but opposition within the revolution gathered force. In a letter to Lenin on 4 March 1920 another of the leading figures of Russian anarchism, the aged prince Peter Kropotkin, argued that 'If the present situation continues, the very word "socialism" will turn into a curse' [97: *256*]. Rather than acting as the banner of the world revolution that would attract socialists from around the world, the experience of communism in Russia discredited the very idea. Not everything was negative, however, and in his 'Message to the Workers of the Western World' of June 1920 Kropotkin sought to look on the positive side of the communist experiment: '[A]lthough the attempt at introducing the new society by means of the dictatorship of one party is apparently doomed to be a failure, it nevertheless must be recognised that the Revolution has already introduced into our everyday life new conceptions about the rights of labour, its true position in society, and the duties of every citizen, which have come to stay' [97: *249*]. However, he stressed that the authoritarian potential within the Bolshevik party predated the ravages of the Civil War and War Communism. 'The evils inherent in party dictatorships have thus been increased by the war conditions under which this party maintained itself. The state of war has been an excuse for strengthening the dictatorial methods of the Party, as well as its tendency to centralise every detail of life in the hands of the government – with the result that immense branches of the usual activities of the nation have been brought to a standstill' [97: *250*]. He ended with a ringing denunciation: '[T]he attempt to build up a communist republic on the lines of a strongly centralised state communism under the iron dictatorship of a party is ending in a failure. We learn in Russia *how communism cannot be introduced*, even though the populations, sick of the old regime, opposed no active resistance to the experiment made by the new rulers' [97: *251*].

The criticisms of the various domestic oppositionists (the very term suggested the existence of an orthodox standard against which the critics tilted) was complemented by perceptive critiques by foreign observers in the socialist tradition. Rosa Luxemburg was on the internationalist wing of German social democracy, and, while she welcomed the Bolshevik revolution as having 'put social- ism on the agenda', from the first she criticised the methods of Leninist rule, above all its suppression of democracy. She insisted that socialism should mean the deepening and not the limitation of democracy, although she understood the need for temporary restrictions. In a famous formulation in 1918 she stressed that 'Freedom only for the supporters of the government, only for members of one party – however numerous they may be – is no freedom at all. Freedom is always and exclusively freedom for the one who thinks differently' [108: *69*]. She played an active part in the German revolution and in January 1919 she was murdered by *Freikorps* officers, demonstrating that the Bolsheviks had no monopoly on civil violence. Kautsky, who as we have seen was one of the leading figures of the German socialist movement, in a pamphlet published in 1918 reaffirmed the commitment of social democracy to parliamentary forms of revolutionary transformation. He insisted that democracy was not only an instrument in the struggle but an inherent component of socialism itself. As he put it, 'For us, therefore, socialism without democracy is unthinkable. We understand by modern socialism not merely social organisation of production, but democratic organisation of society as well' [80: *6*]. To Lenin's fury, he refused to consider the Bolshevik seizure of power as part of the international revolutionary struggle, but regarded it as the outcome of specific Russian conditions, notably the strains of war and relative social underdevelopment.

The French revolution exercised an enduring influence over participants in the Russian revolution in 1917 [82], and France continued to provide the inspiration for models of revolutionary governance. Lenin's only blueprint was the Paris Commune of 1871, which itself was deeply flawed despite Marx's idealistic interpretation of the doomed attempt to create a self-managing egalitarian society. In his romanticised study of the Commune, *The Civil War in France*, Marx condemned the post-revolutionary French state as highly centralised, 'This parasitical excrescence upon civil society', and argued that 'All revolutions thus far only perfected the state machinery instead of throwing off this deadening incubus'. The Russian revolution failed to achieve, and indeed was never intended to be, what Marx had considered the purpose of the Paris Commune, namely 'the revolution against the state itself'. Marx was silent on how the dictatorship of the proletariat would fit into that scheme.

Whereas Marx had considered the 'dictatorship of the proletariat' primarily a social category (although there continues to be a debate about what precisely he meant by the term), Lenin gave the idea a severely political form, meaning the literal dictatorship of one group over another. Marx had first mentioned the idea of the 'dictatorship of the working class' in 1850 to denote the leadership of the workers in relation to the peasants in France, who made up the great majority of the population at the time. As Lovell has stressed, Marx's notion did not exclude a strictly political aspect [107: *69–70*], and Marx was certainly not averse to speaking in terms of revolutionary terror to hasten the overthrow of the decaying old social order, although on many occasions he criticised the historic futility of Jacobin terror. Lenin's understanding of 'dictatorship' stressed the need for unrestrained coercion in the transitional period from socialism, the lower stage of communism, to the higher stage, full-blown communism, where exploitative classes and other enemies of the revolution would have been destroyed. The primitive features of this schema of 'revolutionary temporality' are matched only by the clarity of action they required.

The commune model, moreover, lacked an appreciation of the problem of bureaucracy and regulated institutions for the conduct of politics. Instead, by abolishing the separation of powers and making the Commune 'both executive and legislative', the absence of countervailing powers had a profoundly despotic potential – a potential that was realised half a century later in Russia. In practice the Bolshevik revolution had both a statist and a commune discourse at its heart. The state was to be used to break the economic power of the bourgeoisie and then to develop the country, whereas the commune element was intended to 'smash' the bourgeois state and establish certain principles on which to construct the new one, to prevent the new state becoming a 'supernaturalist abortion of society'. Nevertheless, it was Lenin in *State and Revolution* who reminded readers that in Marx's first stage of socialism the state would have to remain to achieve the transitional tasks (namely, the destruction of the bourgeoisie), a thesis that Stalin took to its logical conclusion.

The model of cohesion implied by the Marxist–Leninist vision of commune democracy was one that was essentially organic, with those within the new political community allegedly united by a single purpose and inspired by the ethos of an emancipated people, while the enemies of the new order would be swept aside mercilessly, a principle that Stalin took to extremes. Stalin had an organicist view of socialism that subordinated individual emancipation to social structures, derived ultimately from Marx's vision of a conflict-free post-revolutionary society. This was an *economistic* view of socialism, stressing the relationship between things (above all the means of production), as opposed to the *humanistic* interpretation, to which Gorbachev later returned, focusing on the quality of relations between people. The Soviet model was based on the myth of social self-identification, to use Leszek Kolakowski's term [87], in which there could be no scope for formal accountability procedures and certainly no need for the separation of powers. Since society was governing itself, what need was there for formal structures of accountability; and would not the separation of powers weaken the revolutionary will of the people? Commune democracy is founded on the belief that, at a certain stage of socialist development, power, conflict and social contestation would, because of the ineluctable laws of historical development, somehow come to an end. It is the opposite of the liberal belief that politics is designed to regulate the naturally occurring and unavoidable conflicts in society. Commune democracy stressed the active participation of citizens, direct democracy and the abolition of the bureaucracy. The myth of harmony, of the socialist part of society, became central, in a modified version of Jean-Jacques Rousseau's theory of the general will, now interpreted by the party. Lenin came to see the state not only as the expression of class rule, but also as the institutionalisation of the management of public affairs.

Marx had spoken of the transcendence (*Aufhebung*) of capitalist society, building on its economic and political achievements, fulfilling the potential of liberalism and capitalism in a post-capitalist society. The democratic potential was to be fulfilled by limiting some of the alleged distortions of liberalism while allowing the liberal promise to be fulfilled – the full development of the individual – something that could not be achieved in capitalist society. In practice, the communist revolutions of the twentieth century did create post-capitalist societies, but, instead of this being a positive transcendence, incorporating all that was best and most dynamic from the old system while eliminating inequality and the exploitative essence of the market system, these revolutions represented what can be called a negative transcendence of capitalism. They did not build on the achievements of capitalism but undermined them, and, instead of being the successors to liberal democracy, acted as its alternative. The revolutions did not fulfil the potential of liberalism but denied the basic aspirations of liberal democracy.

Bolshevism: the Russification of Marxism?

There is a long tradition in the study of the Russian revolution which suggests that the new system represented the continuation of Russian despotic traditions in a communist form. Elements of this argument can be found in Richard Pipes's study of the Russian revolution, in which he stresses the patrimonial traditions in which political and economic power were combined, undermining property rights and political pluralism [127]. In practice matters were not that simple. The Bolshevik seizure of power opened the way for a prolonged clash between a communist (Leninist) civilisation and a Russian civilisation, which retained residual forms of allegiance to traditional patterns of Russian philosophy and behaviour. The Leninist civilisation was based on a transformative modernising programme to be conducted under the aegis of the revolutionary party. It attacked what was perceived to be Russian backwardness, notably through virulent anti-religious campaigns and the destruction of the traditional peasantry, and with it the age-old patterns and structures of village life that Sorokin, for example, had extolled and that Price had described. Nevertheless, although profoundly modified, the bedrock of a distinctive Russian identity, separate and distinct from the Soviet one, survived, and in the end triumphed.

There was a profound interaction between the two civilisations (defined as cultures combining social practices and philosophical orientations), and both were transformed during the course of the short twentieth century, when communism was in power in Russia. Certain motifs, moreover, were common to the two civilisations. For example, communism in secular form redefined the notion of apocalypse, in this case the coming destruction of capitalism to herald the birth of a socially just communist order, while for thinkers like Berdyaev the idea of apocalypse was the distinguishing feature of Russian political philosophy [12]. Equally, Russian history was characterised by repeated bursts of modernisation from above intended, according to Marshall Poe, to sustain a distinctive 'Russian moment in world history'. Poe considers Russia one of the rare civilisations to withstand repeated assaults on its indigenous culture, remaining one of the few non-western paths to modernity [130]. From this perspective Leninist modernisation was no more than a variation on this theme; and the collapse of 1991 reflected a loss of faith in the Russian way that brought to an end an era that long pre-dated Bolshevik power. However, the communist and Russian civilisations did not adequately combine to create a sustainable and durable synthesis, a *Soviet* civilisation that could bear the weight of history. As we shall see, elements of a Soviet civilisation certainly did appear, and it is something which the Communist Party of the Russian Federation (CPRF) in post-communist Russia contemplates with fond regard, but too many elements remained in contradiction, and in the end the whole system collapsed in 1989–91.

The Bolshevik seizure of power in October 1917 contradicted the Marxist schema of revolution in numerous ways. Socialism was assumed to represent the culmination of capitalist progress, when bourgeois production relations acted as a fetter on further development; and the subject of revolution was to be the working class (which by then was to be the majority of the population) emancipating itself from a system that inhibited its development as a class and as individuals, subject to an exploitative and alienating labour process. The Russian revolution met neither of these two conditions. Lenin was well aware of the problem, and, although he may not quite have put it in terms of Russia as the weakest link in the imperialist chain, the Bolshevik seizure of power was predicated on two conditions: that Russia could *start* the revolutionary process that would then have a knock-on effect and bring down the capitalist states of western Europe; and that Russia would *begin* building socialism but it would require the assistance of more mature states to develop appropriately. The apparent absence of a developed working class, moreover, meant that the Bolshevik party acted as the substitute vanguard to make the revolution; and then in due course took the lead in industrial development after the revolution, which according to classic Marxist theory should have been the condition for the revolution itself.

This was the ideological context while Lenin remained alive, but following his death in 1924 Stalin's radical theory of 'socialism in one country', outlined in a series of lectures in that year, repudiated both Leninist conditions. As far as Stalin was concerned, the Soviet Union could not only *begin* the building of socialism, but it could by its own efforts *complete* the process. This represented a massive shift in perspectives, and in effect meant the nationalisation of the international revolution. In practice the Third Communist International (Comintern), created by Lenin in March 1919, had already prioritised Soviet Russian experience and interests; but Stalin made explicit what had been hidden, and made a virtue of what had hitherto been considered an onerous necessity. The socialist revolution had not taken root elsewhere – the German revolution in late 1918 and the Hungarian in 1919 were both defeated – and thus communist Russia was on its own. This isolation enforced reliance on minority dictatorship to retain political power and a bureaucratic class to achieve the regime's economic goals. In the end communist patriotism assumed increasingly Russified forms, pursuing Russian national interests in a communist guise, and thus the whole cycle was completed as the Soviet Union acted as a traditional state. Although paying lip service to international revolution, it repudiated any substantive Marxist transformative agenda.

While Russia had a relatively small working class and economic base on which to try to build an advanced collectivised social order, this does not mean that Marxism was in some way 'Russified', in the sense of fundamentally repudiating basic tenets of the western Marxist tradition. This is also in evidence when it comes to the notion of 'socialism in one country'. Already the German Social Democrats had not denied the possibility of socialism in a single isolated state, and this was in keeping with the widely accepted Marxist notion that capitalism developed unevenly, and that a revolution in one country would have to defend itself until other countries could catch up and help. Marx and Lenin were not opposed to the idea of revolutionary patriotism, and, when it comes to Stalinist foreign policy, Marx and Engels had always conceived of world revolution taking the form of interstate conflict, accompanied of course by domestic civil war (184).

The practice of Bolshevism in power, moreover, contradicted much of what socialists had long dreamed, and certainly stood in opposition to broad layers of the Russian revolution. The system was massively coercive from the very first, and this feature gained in intensity, with occasional pauses, and culminated in the great terror of the 1930s. The Kadets and other 'bourgeois' parties were outlawed in the days following the revolution, and the press was from the first severely controlled by the Bolsheviks. The Mensheviks refused to declare themselves in outright opposition to the Bolsheviks and thus retained a lingering presence in the soviets until their destruction in the early 1920s, while in the first 'show trial' in 1922 the SR leadership was executed and imprisoned. The Cheka from the first imposed the death penalty not only as a punitive sanction but also as a prophylactic, in which class status was enough to be shot. It was under Lenin that the first concentration camps were created, famously in the Solovetskii monastery in the White Sea, renamed 'correctional-labour camps' in 1931. The first occupants were the non-Bolshevik revolutionaries, notably the agrarian-based SRs and anarchists, joined of course by various 'white guardists' and anti-revolutionaries ranging from monarchists to constitutional democrats.

Any social project will take native forms as it adapts to circumstances, but the idea that communism in Russia was a degenerate form of world communism as a result of its Russification is questionable. The negative transcendence of capitalism led to the creation of an uncivil society, and the roots of this lay not only in the way that the theory was implemented (and the theory in the first instance was far more ambiguous than the partisans of Russian degeneration would suggest). The Marxist–Leninist regime in the Soviet Union radically denied elements of contract in the relationship between state and society. Relations were indeed transparent, with a powerful state and a society that lacked autonomous sources of political organisation. The abolition of the market entailed the abolition of the distinction between the state and civil society, and the direct politicisation of socio-economic relationships dispensed with political pluralism even within the revolution while enhancing the powers of the bureaucratic class. In the Marxist–Leninist version, the general will after the establishment of the social contract, which they called the proletarian revolution was determined by the communist party, and this claim to a privileged relationship to the truth of socialism imposed a fateful rift between socialism and democracy, and meant that Bolshevism represented a coup against the rest of the Russian movement for social change. The revolution that was proclaimed to put an end to autocratic power and alienation created a system that intensified despotism.

3 Stalinism and Communist Reform

The New Economic Policy represented the abandonment (temporarily) of the 'revolutionary' strategy of War Communism in favour of a 'reformist' approach, but this reformism was of a distinctive and highly ambivalent sort. It was a tactical rather than a strategic retreat. As Lenin put it, NEP 'would last a long time but not forever'. How long 'long' would be was not defined, and in 1928–9 the regime once again went on the offensive. Communism in Russia remained a type of crusade, with a two-fold project designed to transform its own society and the individuals who composed it, while at the same time calling for revolutionary change in the world at large. The tension between involution, the adaptation of a transformative agenda into the inward-looking maintenance of an existing order, and revolution was to remain until the end. When this tension disappeared and world revolution was abandoned, in both rhetoric and practice, the domestic order also dissolved.

Stalin's revolution from above

In the jockeying for power that followed Lenin's death in January 1924, Stalin proved the most adept at exploiting the fissures in the regime to secure his power against Trotsky, Bukharin and other Bolshevik leaders. At first Stalin supported Bukharin's moderate policies within the framework of NEP, but by the late 1920s, despite the evident success of NEP in restoring industry and prosperity to the countryside, sought ways to go beyond its limitations. The regime was effectively hostage to the peasants' willingness to sell grain on the market. At the same time, already in 1924 Stalin had announced the idea of 'socialism in one country', modifying Lenin's internationalism and establishing the priority of Soviet state interests against those of the international revolution. As noted, Stalin insisted that Russia could not only *begin* the transition to socialism, but could go on to *complete* its construction by its own efforts. The countryside would have to pay for the investment required.

Stalin's rise to supreme power was due not only to his skilful exploitation of bureaucratic mechanisms, but perhaps above all to the political opportunism and incompetence of his main rivals (with the notable exception of Bukharin). Trotsky's challenge for the leadership, and even his attempts to retain a voice in the post-Leninist order, were unprepared, impulsive and politically incoherent. Stalin's letters to Molotov demonstrate that his defeat of Trotsky in debates within the Politburo greatly augmented his authority and allowed him to consolidate power [106]. In other words, Trotsky was the author of his own (and others') downfall. While Tucker argued that Stalin destroyed what was left of Bolshevism, Lenin had already reduced the revolutionary socialist and even the Bolshevik tradition to an eviscerated dogma that was hostile to independent thought, intolerant of diversity and punitive against internal and external opponents.

Artificial forms of class struggle were imposed on the countryside, with the poor peasants allegedly exploiting the so-called rich peasants (the *kulaks*), but in fact collectivisation entailed a massive exercise of urban power over the countryside. Stalin's revolution from above was directed initially against the peasantry, forcing them into collective farms (*kolkhozy*), making it easier to extract grain in order to fund industrialisation. Stalin's decree of 30 January 1930 ordered the liquidation of the kulaks as a class 'by confining them in concentration camps, not hesitating to carry out the highest measure of repression [execution]', with district troikas 'to examine cases and pass sentences quickly without investigation'. Millions of the most successful peasants were exiled to the north and east, and the new collective farms struggled for years to restore production. Peasants were in effect reduced to a new form of serfdom.

The five-year plans for industrialisation were launched within the framework of the state planning agency, Gosplan. The principles of command and administer were now applied to every aspect of economic and social life, including the arts and personal life. The traditional view is that collectivisation made an essential contribution to the financing of ambitious industrialisation targets as laid out in the First Five-Year Plan, adopted in 1928 [119]. Forced collectivisation, in which some 5 million peasants died, provoked a huge loss in traction power (primarily horses) and livestock, and it is unclear whether any substantial surplus really was generated. The aim was as much political as it was economic – to remove one of the last remaining 'veto players' (the peasantry) from the political scene.

In Ukraine, the Kuban and the lower Volga from 1932 famine became widespread, which from 1933 in Ukraine took the intense form that is today known as the *Golodomor* (*Holodomor* in Ukrainian), the alleged deliberate genocide conducted against Ukraine by the Moscow authorities. Evidence that this was genocide is uncertain, since Russian parts of the south also suffered and some food reserves were diverted to the region. Even without nationalist discourses it is clear that Stalinism at this time represented a war against the peasantry as a group, but Stalin's decisions in autumn 1932 turned the famine into an instrument of national policy. Equally, it is uncertain how deliberate was the famine in Kazakhstan in 1930–2, but we do know that some 1.3–1.5 million Kazakhs, hitherto a nomadic people but now forced to settle in collective farms, died of starvation, over 30 per cent of the indigenous population. The Nazis soon discovered that the collective farm was a magnificent instrument of exploitation, and, despite the hopes of Ukrainian nationalists that the Germans would restore peasant holdings, the *kolkhozy* were kept in the occupied areas after June 1941. The countryside has still not recovered from collectivisation across large parts of what had been the Soviet Union.

Observers were enthusiastic about the onset of Stalin's 'third revolution', the launching of the collectivisation drive that would once and for all put an end to capitalism in Russia. Arthur Koestler enthused about the associated acceleration of industrialisation through the five-year plans: 'On one sixth of our sick planet, the most gigantic constructive effort of all times had begun; there Utopia was being built in steel and concrete' [86: *245*]. For Koestler this represented 'the Great Experiment' [86: *227*].

The Comintern, based in Moscow as the headquarters of the world revolution, discredited itself by failing to recognise the danger posed by Adolf Hitler's Nazi party in Germany. In the so-called 'third period' between 1928 and 1935 the Comintern pursued an ultra-left militant line on the assumption that capitalism was entering its death agonies, and thus failed to unite with German Social Democrats to block Hitler's rise. The Seventh Comintern Congress in 1935 finally opened the door to alliances and endorsed the idea of a 'popular front' against fascism. Against the background of world depression communist sentiments may have been on the rise in the 1930s, but so were extreme right-wing ideologies. The Spanish Civil War from 1936 to 1939, in which the legitimate Republican government (aided by the Soviet Union) was defeated by an insurgency led by General Francisco Franco (aided by the Axis powers, Germany and Italy), epitomised the polarised politics of the era. It served as the prologue to the Second World War and added international threats to accentuate Stalin's customary paranoia.

The power of the secret police climaxed in the purges and great terror of 1937–8. The infamous order No. 00447 of 5 August 1937 laid the basis for quotas for the arrest of 'anti-Soviet elements', with an initial four-month target of 268,950 people, divided by regions, of whom about a third were to be executed. The great purges represented a spectacular case of state terrorism, with terror defined as attacks against civilians, in this case its own. The ramified and arbitrary nature of Stalin's purges remains a conundrum. State terror is usually intended to send a message to society to desist from perceived subversive activities, but the sheer scale of the Russian events makes it far more than this. The scale of the Soviet slaughter of its own people is astounding, with a total of at least 5 million killed in the period from 1928 to 1953. In those years some 30 million were sent to the *gulag*, the term used by Solzhenitsyn to describe the great archipelago of labour camps that stretched across the country, of whom some 3 million died.

At the height of the great terror in 1937–8 at least 1,372,392 people were arrested, of whom 681,692 were shot [28]. The largest single category at that time was the 'kulaks', who had already been repressed earlier, and now 386,798 were killed. The next largest group was the ethnic Poles who were Soviet citizens, of whom, in a foretaste of the massacre of 22,000 Polish officers and reservists at Katyn and four other sites in spring 1940, 111,091 were shot. In fact, ethnic minorities contributed a third of the total of deaths, even though the affected groups comprised only 2 per cent of the Soviet population. The purge of the communist party elite, to which so much attention has been devoted, claimed 'only' 47,737 lives, notably the 'old Bolsheviks', those who had created the system that in the end devoured them [161]. The gulag system of labour camps spread like an amoeba across the country, devouring millions who were deployed to develop the harsh northern regions such as the coalfields in Vorkuta and the Komi Republic or the gold and platinum deposits in the Kolyma region. In the end, even Soviet leaders realised that the high mortality rate was unsustainable, and from 1939, when Lavrenty Beria was appointed head of the gulag empire, rations and medical care were improved: not out of any humanitarian concerns but from the realisation that healthy labourers would work better than sick ones [3].

Mass violence was a central characteristic of the first part of the twentieth century, termed 'democide' by Rummel [146], a type of genocide in which the authorities turn against their own people. This was certainly 'lethal politics' with a vengeance. Russian terrorism had its roots in the 1870s, combining a primitive logic of struggle with a collapse of moral categories, while a large part of 'educated society' ranged themselves on the side of the terrorists; but from the very first socialists such as Plekhanov warned that terror for genuine revolutionaries was both unjustified and counter-productive, and thus he found himself isolated in 1917. The scale and forms of Bolshevik terror were something new for Russia. The census of 6 January 1937 found that the Soviet population amounted to 162 million, at least 10 million lower than would have been expected if natural demographic tendencies had operated. The Soviet authorities declared the result 'defective and damaging' (*vreditel'skim*) and swiftly classified the information, while repressing the census-takers.

On the eve of the war Stalin dealt the Soviet Union an almost mortal self-inflicted blow by striking down over three-quarters of the Soviet High Command and the officer elite. Victims in 1937–8 included Marshal Mikhail Tukhachevsky, one of the most talented Soviet officers, but one whose warnings about the danger emanating from Nazi Germany irritated Stalin. The victims were random, often the object of anonymous denunciations as neighbours sought a few extra metres of living space. The chains of conspiracy and denunciation caught up relatives and friends in arbitrary patterns, with names often chosen to fulfil the local police quotas. The leadership of the NKVD itself was periodically purged: Genrikh Yagoda in 1937 gave way to Nikolai Yezhov, who himself fell victim in 1939 and was replaced by Beria, who put an end to the first phase of the great terror. At the same time, as Wheatcroft has recently demonstrated [190], there was remarkable continuity in membership of the core group responsible for the killing during the Civil War, collectivisation and the great terror. According to Alexander Yakovlev, one of the architects of perestroika who headed a presidential commission on the rehabilitation of political repression victims, over 2,000 writers and poets died in the purges between the 1917 Bolshevik revolution and the death of Stalin in 1953. Most of the intellectuals either starved to death in prison camps or were executed. Political repression continued in the years after Stalin's death, but with a much reduced intensity. Under Brezhnev, more than 150 writers, musicians, composers and artists were exiled to foreign countries.

The search for a rational explanation of the purges remains. Hiroaki Kuromiya argues that the core purpose of the mass terror was to launch 'a pre-emptive strike to prepare for war' [100: *3*]. According to Rittersporn, one of the factors was Stalin's fear of the personalisation of political relations that threatened his own pre-eminence [144]. Ideas were important for Stalin, and the great terror is seen as the culmination of a 'revivalist' mobilisation campaign against 'class aliens', 'internal disbelievers', and 'fifth columnist members of diaspora nationalities' [135: *309*]. Drawing on what he identifies as a tension in Marx's thinking, Priestland distinguishes between romantic and technocratic approaches to modernisation, with the latter focusing more on material incentives and rational self-interests, as propounded by Bukharin in the 1920s and Deng Xiaoping in post-Mao China. The division between communists who relied on economic processes and science versus a belief in revolutionary consciousness and proletarian energy is one that fractures all revolutionary movements, and was evident within Bolshevism from the very first. Lenin always inclined to the former, and by 1920 explicitly prioritised routine and development over revolutionary enthusiasm. As a 'revivalist', Stalin was concerned with ideological unity and commitment, and in this respect prefigures Mao Zedong's revivalism of the Cultural Revolution. Indeed, the parallels between the Chinese and Russian revolutions are probably deeper than exponents of the 'national characteristics' school of Chinese studies allow. Equally, as Zygmunt Bauman has argued, the Holocaust was not specifically a product of Nazism or a confluence of uniquely evil people but emerged out of modern bureaucratic organisation, in which hierarchical obedience is prized and in which the actions of one layer are partially obscured by others [10], and this applies also to the Soviet terror.

Soviet mass murder, like the German variant, was indeed accompanied by a pedantic bureaucratism and the endless filling of folders and files. Stalin, however, was well aware of the limits of what he could control. As a study by Getty and Naumov makes clear in tracing the rise of Yezhov, at the head of the NKVD at the height of the terror, Stalin was unable to control the whole flow of information and was in no position to decide everything, and thus there was some scope for his subordinates to shape their own agendas. Indeed, the authors argue that even as late as 1936 the erratic policy changes reveal 'indecision, false starts, contradictions, short-term improvisation' as Stalin's typical working style [57: *212*] Yezhov was useful to Stalin because of his dogged loyalty as well as his modest lifestyle, compared with the extravagance of his predecessor, Yagoda, who had built himself a palatial dacha filled with luxuries. Yezhov was convinced that he was furthering the cause of the revolution, drawing on the profoundly axiological thinking that had characterised Bolshevik culture from even before the revolution, permeated by simple binaries of 'us' and 'them', which in the Civil War was implemented as the practice of 'kill or be killed', and now meant the liquidation of potential enemies. For Yezhov freedom consisted 'of silencing the voices of those who opposed the struggles of workers, soldiers and peasants' [57: *223*], and in his view the country's problems were caused by 'ill-intentioned people, by enemies of the people' [57: *224*]. Those who obstructed the building of a happy world for the workers were not just mistaken but evil and had to be eliminated.

Stalin was more than the 'grey blur' suggested by Trotsky. He was an intelligent and able politician in the Leninist mould, for whom ideas remained important. Although Marxist philosophy is based on a materialist conception of history, recent studies have demonstrated that Stalin remained something of an idealist, in the sense that for him ideas could take on an almost material reality [184]. Indeed, Stalin considered himself something of a scholar, and took a keen interest in various academic controversies, notably in Trofim Lysenko's assertion of control over biology in 1948 and the debate at that time over the possibility of a 'Marxist physics', and he contributed a major work on linguistics just before his death, comparable in its wrong-headedness to Lenin's *Materialism and Empirio-Criticism* of 1908. While Lysenko set back Soviet genetics by two decades, scientists with Beria's help were able to maintain the autonomy of physics as they raced to build the Soviet atom bomb. The centrality of ideas meant that Stalinist terror sought to crush not only actions that could pose a danger to the regime but also thoughts that could threaten the socialist state. This is a logic that was apparent in other great revolutions. Following the frenzy of freedom in 1789, the French revolution soon began to devour itself in the Jacobin terror where 'thought crimes' were considered as threatening as counter-revolutionary activity; and the bearers of these crimes were understandably pre-eminently found among the ranks of the revolutionaries themselves.

Khlevniuk argues that the Soviet system alternated between periods of oligarchic and dictatorial rule. For most of its existence the Soviet system was oligarchic, but in the period between 1935 and 1953 Stalin exercised dictatorial power. He finds no evidence of factional conflict in this period, or even that a division between radicals and moderates is warranted. Individuals lined up depending on the issue under discussion, and thus the view that Sergo Ordzhonikidze or Valeryan Kuibyshev was a potential leader of a more moderate wing that might in due course have challenged Stalin is discounted. Equally, Khlevniuk [85] argues that there is no evidence that Kirov received more votes than Stalin in elections to the Politburo at the Seventeenth Party Congress in 1934, or that Stalin planned Kirov's murder on 1 December of that year, the event that sparked in due course the great terror. Certainly Stalin used the ensuing purges to settle scores with the old Bolsheviks, those senior leaders in the Party who had worked with Lenin, and thus ended the base for oligarchic politics, with their accompanying debates over policy matters, and assumed undivided and unchallenged supremacy. This was formalised in 1935 when Stalin abolished the post of 'second' Party secretary, held at the time by his long-time colleague Lazar Kaganovich. Throughout Stalin took care to ensure that no individual accumulated too much power, a stricture that even applied to his loyal henchman Vyacheslav Molotov. From 1930 Molotov was chair of Sovnarkom (effectively prime minister), and only on 6 May 1941 did Stalin take over Lenin's old post, in addition to remaining first secretary of the party.

Stalin asserted that 'cadres decide everything', but this did not mean independent decision-making for individuals. In practice, local and regional networks emerged, enjoying reciprocal support relationships that subverted instructions from the centre. Webs of clientelistic relations took shape that blossomed in the post-Stalin era [191]. Planning became little more than an exercise in book-keeping, with ever more complex plan indicators circumvented by ever more sophisticated stratagems by enterprises. Nevertheless, the rudiments of a modern industrial economy were built, although at great cost. The distortions of the Stalinist command economy, the destruction of the most active people in the countryside, the neglect of the service sector, the reduction of money to an internal accounting unit, and the relative isolation of the Soviet economy from world development burdened post-Stalin Russia with severe structural problems.

While profoundly flawed because of its static descriptive approach, the notion of totalitarianism nevertheless tries to ask the right questions: namely, how can we explain the phenomenon of the grotesque expansion of state aspirations, and in many cases real power, in the twentieth century? Historians of Nazi Germany have demonstrated the sophistication of the regime, and use the notion of totalitarianism only to demonstrate its limited applicability to German conditions. The *Historikerstreit* (historians' controversy) from 1986 tried a new tack in attempting to find the causality and links between Soviet and German hyper-authoritarianism (if not totalitarianism) in the twentieth century. Ernst Nolte examined the history of Bolshevism, the USSR, National Socialism and the Third Reich in the context of what he argued was a European civil war. This war, he asserted, was ideologically justified by the Bolshevik government in Russia, supported by the Communist Party of Germany. In other words, Nolte argued that Nazi atrocities were in part a response to earlier Bolshevik crimes, and were thus neither unique nor a specific attribute of German history. By contextualizing the history of the Third Reich in the framework of broader developments in twentieth century European history, and in particular the Bolshevik revolution and Stalin's rule, he inevitably relativised the German regime's atrocities and thus to a degree exculpated its crimes [117]. We shall return to the problem of totalitarianism in the final chapter.

In reaction to the 'from above' historiography of the totalitarian model, a new wave of social historians began to write the history of Stalinism 'from below'. In various works Sheila Fitzpatrick stressed that traditional approaches emphasising the role of the state, or which apply the totalitarian model, neglect important social processes, and thus society is reduced to an 'undifferenti-ated whole' [47: *359*]. There were always limits, if not formally constituted, to Stalin's power. This has provided rich studies of the way that central policies were transformed when applied by lower-level functionaries and blunted by social practices. At its best this was far more than 'history with the politics left out' [44: *385–94*], although the new social history, which became such a powerful tendency just as the Soviet regime entered its death throes, focused on elements of stability and permanence and obscured deeper questions about the philosophical–politi-cal character of the regime. A further criticism of 'revisionist' approaches is their alleged lack of theoretical content, although the mining of a rich seam of empirical material added much to our understanding of how the Soviet system actually worked. It was not that revisionism was under-theorised, but that its under-standing of such key issues as 'power' took a more complex view than simple traditional notions of domination and acquiescence [48; 159]. There was a tendency, however, to lose sight of the wood amongst the trees.

Russia and war

In response to the Boxer uprising in China, in 1901 Russian, Japanese, German, French and American forces combined to defeat the popular insurgency against western dominance. In the rest of the century Russia (in its various guises) was in turn in conflict with each of them. In 1904 Russia went to war with Japan over Manchuria, only to suffer one defeat after another and the 1905 revolution. In 1914 it was Germany's turn as Russia once again went to war, this time in defence of Serbia. Defeat on this occasion turned into disaster for the regime in 1917. Contrary to what Lenin had anticipated, the seizure of power by the proletariat in Russia did not herald a general world revolu-tion. In his April Theses of 1917 Lenin had tied the fate of Russia to 'world revolution'; Soviet Russia was to be no more than a bridgehead for the spread of revolutionary socialist ideas. The domestic policies of the USSR were fundamentally shaped by the global perspective of the Soviet state and in particular by its ideological commitment to communism as an international phenomenon. This helps explain Stalinist industrialisation and collectivisation. Although the revolutionary impulse was tempered by domestic involution, no stable relationship was found between the Soviet Union and the international community, although direct warfare was confined to the period of the Second World War, once again primarily against Germany although in the end also against Japan. The Cold War between 1947 and 1989, despite various phases of *Ostpolitik*, détente and rapprochement, saw the Soviet Union ranged alone against all of its erstwhile allies of 1901. The century ended in 1999 with Russia lined up against all nineteen members of NATO over the latter's bombing of Serbia.

In the run-up to the Second World War, Stalin's motives have been much debated: was his purpose primarily defensive or was there a deeper expansionist aspiration in his policies? The acceptance of Hitler's offer of a mutual division of eastern Europe in late August 1939 (the Nazi–Soviet Pact of 23 August), according to Raack, was about more than territory; it was to act as the spark to provoke a Europe-wide revolution [137]. The evidence for this is contentious, and Stalin's policy at this time, as it probably was in the immediate post-war years, was guided more by opportunism than the fulfilment of a deep-laid plan. The web of deception surrounding the onset of the Nazi–Soviet war in 1941 still remains to be unveiled [9].

The Soviet economy, with all its flaws, nevertheless provided the sinews of might to defeat the Nazi German invasion of 22 June 1941. The war was fought primarily as a *national* struggle for survival, symbolised by the dissolution of Comintern in May 1943. Specifically Russian traditions were revived, including elements of imperial insignia, and it looked as if the gulf between the Russian and Soviet civilisations would be transcended. The USSR emerged victorious in May 1945 as part of the winning alliance with the western powers. This unity soon crumbled into the Cold War as it became clear that Soviet power had come to stay in the eastern European countries liberated from fascism by the Red Army, but now to be subordinated to the great Soviet communist experiment. The victory was a sour one: as Lev Kopelev put it, 'the deserved defeat of the Hitlerites became the undeserved triumph of the Stalinists' [90]. The way was opened to the emergence of Stalinist Soviet chauvinism, an endless arms race, and the militarisation of Soviet society and the economy that in the end brought the country to its knees.

Just as the number of victims of the great terror and associated catastrophes remain controversial, so too estimates of Soviet losses in the war have been the subject of political speculation. The figure of 7 million Soviet losses in the war was first introduced by Stalin in February 1945, but how he derived this figure is unclear, since even at that time the estimated losses were considered far higher. The British representative in Berne in March 1945, for example, suggested a figure of 30 million. Stalin reduced the figures, fearing that excessively high losses would reduce the USSR's international prestige and cast doubt on the competence of his leadership. Stalin's figure was comparable to the German losses, which in 1945 were estimated to total 6–6.5 million, of which 4–4.5 million were military losses, figures that have barely changed to this day. In the early 1960s, however, Khrushchev introduced the figure of 20 million, a number that corresponded to the preponderance of women in the Soviet population according to the 1959 census. A decade and a half after the war, this figure could not be an accurate indicator of military losses. For Khrushchev the figure was intended to demonstrate the incompetence of the Soviet leadership under Stalin. Following Khrushchev's ousting in 1964 his successors stuck to the figure of 20 million, but now to illustrate the sufferings of the Soviet people as a result of Nazi aggression and to demonstrate the huge Soviet contribution to victory, and thereby to legitimate the Soviet presence in eastern Europe. In the early Gorbachev years the figure once again changed, and in 1989 was raised to 26.6 million, the figure that remains the official estimate today, with the official figure for military losses raised to 8.86 million in 2007. Although the *glasnost'* (openness) of the perestroika period did fill in many of the 'blank spots' in the Soviet past, the new figure once again had a political motive; to appeal to the western public and to show the sacrifices that its former ally had made in the joint struggle against Nazi Germany, and thus to delegitimate the continuance of the Cold War. About one in twenty-five Russian civilians were killed by the Germans during the war, about one in ten Ukrainians, and an astonishing one in five Belarusians [161].

What did Russia gain through all of its wars and conflicts? The grandeur of victory over Nazi Germany cannot be gainsaid, but the foundations of the Soviet state were undermined. The deportation of whole peoples within the Soviet Union set a time bomb ticking in nationality relations: the 1.2 million Volga Germans, the Chechens, Ingush, the Crimean Tatars, the Kalmyks, followed then by the deportation of millions of German inhabitants from East Prussia, Silesia and the Sudetenland. The USSR was the only state that gained substantial territory as a result of the war: between 1939 and 1940, in alliance with Germany, it acquired the Baltic republics, western Belorussia, western Ukraine, Bukovina, Bessarabia and some Finnish territories, and then in 1944–5, in conjunction with the Allied powers, the previous gains were supplemented by East Prussia (now the exclave of Kaliningrad), Transcarpathian Ukraine, Pechenga district, South Sakhalin and the four south-ernmost Kurile Islands, the latter souring relations with Japan to this day. In 1944 the territory of Tuva in the Russian Far East, which had maintained a precarious independence as a separate state since 1922, 'voluntarily united' with the Soviet Union. The Great Patriotic War for Russia ended in 1944 with the liberation of its territory, and thereafter the advance towards Berlin turned into a war of conquest.

Although the Soviet Union won the war, it lost the peace. Although in technical terms the USSR rebuilt remarkably quickly, the country never really recovered the expenditure in personnel and resources. Hopes for those returning from the fronts that life would be freer and that fear of the secret police and purges would be removed were disappointed, and instead the Stalinist dictator-ship returned, although perhaps not quite as ferocious as in the pre-war years. Reconciliation between the people and power was possible in 1945, and thus dual Russia could have been overcome. Instead the communist regime reasserted its privileged position and thus missed a unique moment when adaptation to the aspirations of society would not necessarily have meant the self-liquidation of the system. The war acted as a long shadow over the final Soviet decades, a shadow that became deeper as the years passed. With few other achievements, the war became the only genuinely resonant foundation myth amidst the sea of communist propaganda.

The limits of reform communism

Stalin's death on 5 March 1953 left his successors with major dilemmas. The country had been governed by the dictatorial rule of a morbidly suspicious leader for several decades, and the institutions of governance, including the Communist Party of the Soviet Union (CPSU), as the party was renamed in 1952, had been reduced to little more than an instrument to provide legitimacy to one-man rule. Stalinist command methods were clearly stifling innovation and preventing the economic system from moving beyond the primary phase of industrialisation to intensive methods in which more complex and technologically sophisticated practices could apply. The idea of reform haunted the Khrushchev period and reflected recognition of the inadequacies of the Stalinist model, but 'reform communism' (the attempt genuinely to humanise and democratise the communist dictatorship) remained limited and partial up to 1985.

In his 'Secret Speech' that began just before midnight on 24 February 1956 at the Twentieth Party Congress Khrushchev began to lift the lid on some of Stalin's crimes, including the deportation of whole peoples in 1944 (the Chechens, the Ingush, the Balkars and others). Destalinisation recognised the need for change, but it was also an attempt to limit the change to a condemnation of the man, Joseph Stalin, and not of the system that had allowed such a man to terrorise his own population for so long. Destalinisation was bound up with personal conflict within the Soviet leadership. The year after the Twentieth Congress Khrushchev denounced the so-called 'anti-party group' of alleged Stalin sympathisers, even though one of them, Dmitry Shepilov, had helped Khrushchev draft his secret speech [158].

While the policies espoused by Imre Nagy in Hungary in 1956 and later by intellectuals in eastern Europe focused on Marxist reformism, Khrushchev's sought to generate a programme of Leninist reformism, a theme that Gorbachev took up in the early phase of perestroika. It soon became clear that any reform strategy based on Leninism would become intellectually and politically exhausted, since Leninism was too slender a theory to bear the philosophical weight of a programme of 'reform communism'. Reform communism is a programme that seeks to reinvigorate Soviet-type systems while remaining loyal to the fundamental principles of

79

Marxism–Leninism as applied in the Soviet Union, whereas communist reform was potentially a more open-ended process, entailing the adaptation of communist regimes to the society in which they found themselves. Thus the Hungarian revolution in 1956 is an example of communist reform (with an open-ended outcome that by the end became increasingly radical), whereas the Prague Spring in 1968 under Alexander Dubček and Gorbachev's perestroika were classic cases of reform communism, although both by the end were becoming the reform of communism.

Communist reform allows a regime to adapt to society, whereas reform communism retains at least a residual vanguardism. In the end, however, it turned out that Leninism's political practices had been too primitive, and its ideology too circumscribed by the logic of seizing and holding on to power, to have much use to those who sought to modernise communism. This was a lesson that Gorbachev, too, would learn a generation later. In the event Khrushchev's reforms, conducted under the slogan of returning to the alleged original purity of the revolution under Lenin, were deeply ambiguous and flawed, if for no other reason than that (as we have seen) the October revolution consisted of many levels that were in tension with each other. There was no original grail of pure and unadulterated socialism to which Stalin's successors could return, as Gorbachev was to discover. Khrushchev's erratic style of rule, moreover, so thoroughly alarmed the defenders of the elite that in October 1964 they ousted him.

The long rule (1964–82) of Leonid Brezhnev was a period of retrenchment and conservative reaction, but some of the key features of the Khrushchev era were maintained. Support for agriculture and the attempt to shift from producer to consumer goods remained priorities. However, most of the institutional innovations of the Khrushchev era, such as the decentralisation initiative in creating some 100 regional economic councils (*sovnarkhozy*) in an attempt to improve economic coordination, and initiatives to stimulate popular participation, were reversed. The centralised ministries were restored and the rule of local party committees was consolidated. The 'stability of cadres' policy effectively gave officials jobs for life, but fostered complacency and corruption. Extensive patronage networks ultimately even came to challenge the prerogatives of the party in making personal appointments (the *nomenklatura* system). Under Brezhnev not only did economic growth slow but the polity itself began to fragment. Party bosses in the regions set themselves up as local barons, developing patronage and clientelist networks that undermined the authority of official party channels. In the national republics this localism took on an ethnic element, with the titular nationality privileged by taking the top jobs. The Soviet modernisation programme created a growing class of managers, educationalists and so on who represented a proto-middle class, yet their evolution into a class not only of themselves but also for themselves, a self-confident bourgeoisie ready to demand and defend their rights, was circumscribed by the regime's attempt to maintain, if only residually, a proletarian class identity.

The Brezhnev era was a classic period of *bezvremen'e* (literally timelessness), which can be interpreted in a double sense: first as hard times, and second, as a period of social stagnation. The Brezhnev era has been characterised by the notion of a 'neo-Stalinist contract', based on an implicit deal between the regime and the people. The regime promised improved standards of living, housing, and so on, and in return the population was not to make political demands on the system. Neo-Stalinism was an unsocial contract in that it was imposed from above. Whereas for Hobbes there was a voluntary renunciation of rights for the greater good, in the unsocial contract there was no bargaining between equals, and no residual rights remained with the individual. The delegation of sovereignty in Hobbes remained partial, whereas in the USSR the alienation of sovereignty was total. Hence the neo-Stalinist social contract was paternalistic and infantilising.

The Brezhnev years saw the Soviet system at its most 'normal', with no system-threatening external or internal threats. The challenge represented by the 'Prague Spring' of 1968 to democratise Soviet-style communism by introducing 'socialism with a human face', where the party's right to rule was to be achieved through effective policies and not to be derived in perpetuity from the very act of seizing power, was crushed by the Soviet-led Warsaw Pact invasion of 20–21 August 1968. The destruction of reform communism in Czechoslovakia was followed by a period of 'normalisation' in which thousands of reformers were expelled from the communist party; and the stifling of sources of innovation and dynamism was carried over into Soviet domestic policy. Henry Kissinger reportedly was pleased that the Prague Spring came to an end, since it demonstrated that there was no alternative to capitalism;

it also demonstrated that there was no permissible alternative to Leninist socialism [17]. Indeed, learning from the reform of communism in Hungary in 1956, the Czechoslovak leadership sought to limit change to reform communism, although in a radical form, but even this was too much for the Soviet leadership.

Soviet renewal and 'dissent' were persecuted with single-minded ruthlessness by Yuri Andropov, at the head of the KGB from 1967. Although the system became less repressive than it had been under Stalin, it was no less intrusive in trying to shape the appropriate behaviour of communists, and indeed to create a 'new socialist man', with endless exhortations that affected even the most intimate details of personal lives. The coming together (*sblizhenie*) of Leninist communism and Russian characteristics (of which collectivism was just one) was creating a new Soviet civilisation; but this was a civilisation based on daily practices and a way of life that was not allowed to gain genuine political institutions. Thus 'Soviet civilisation' was unable to take a political form. Soviet-style communism was condemned now to an extended period of entropy, with no self-sustaining mechanism of growth or regeneration allowed to revitalise the system. The neo-Stalinist 'contract' now became entrenched, whereby the regime made the implicit promise that, in exchange for increased standards of living and non-interference in private life, the public would not make political demands of the system and would keep its views to itself. A type of neo-Stalinism was restored, without mass terror but where the suffocating rule of the petty bureaucracy inhibited initiative and imbued the whole era with an aura of immobility.

Domestic stagnation at home was partially offset by dynamism abroad. The policy of détente in the 1970s partially opened the country to the West, yet ultimately détente only intensified domestic stagnation. The system increasingly began to take on neo-feudal elements. What else was the system to do other than perpetuate itself, which became an increasingly solipsistic exercise? The source of Brezhnevian timelessness and stagnation was the death of the future and the idea of progress. A movement dedicated to the creation of a bright future had been given licence to be irresponsible and wanton in the destruction of the past and unrealistic in appraising the present. Now this irresponsibility in terms of human lives and resources began to catch up with the system. Brezhnev's rule saw the death of utopianism and the narrowing of the socialist project. A future-oriented project now lost control over *telos*, and thus its ability to shape the *logos* also waned. The Soviet system had nothing left to offer the people; hence it became stagnant. The enormous effort to maintain manual control over the polity and to energise the economy ran out of steam.

Brezhnev's death in November 1982 provided his successor, Andropov, with the opportunity to experiment with ways of regenerating the system. In keeping with his long years at the head of the KGB, his approach was that of 'authoritarian modernisation', employing the heavy-handed tactics of the secret policeman to defeat corruption and to kick-start the engine of economic growth. Andropov tried unsuccessfully to combine discipline and reform. Fate, however, intervened to cut Andropov's innovations short, and his death in February 1983 allowed Konstantin Chernenko, one of the worst, oldest and most complacent of Brezhnev's acolytes, a brief period to pretend to rule before his own death in March 1985 inaugurated an exhilarating period of change.

One of the key features of Stalinism was the tacit pact made with the criminal (*blatnoi*) world. At its crudest, this was seen in the labour camps, where criminal *zeks* were given power to terrorise political prisoners, a feature described by Solzhenitsyn in his *The Gulag Archipelago*. Under Khrushchev and Brezhnev this became a whole system of tacit agreements delineating spheres of influence. During the *Andropovshchina* criminals were unleashed to inflict the torture that the official system was afraid to do. The anti-alcohol campaign and the encouragement of hybrid co-operatives during perestroika proved an ideal climate for the criminal mafia to come to the surface of Soviet life. This bargain with the underworld was in some respects similar to the one Vera Dunham identified between Stalin and the new Soviet middle classes in the form of what she called the 'big deal' [40]. By the time of Brezhnev a whole criminal underground world had emerged with its own songs and publications (*blatizdat*). The 'mafia' in certain areas began to fuse with the party itself, especially in Uzbekistan. Thus began the process of retreat of the Soviet state, leaving behind it a poisoned social terrain for the post-communist state to deal with. It was not accidental that the *blatnoi* world should have been the first to be uncovered by the retreat of the glacier of Soviet power. The two worlds were alike in many ways and operated according to conventions and mores that were often interchangeable.

Nation and adaptation

In his pamphlet of 1916 *The Socialist Revolution and the Right of Nations to Self-Determination*, Lenin called for the self-determination for peoples as way of breaking up the multinational empires that dominated the world at that time, but he drew on the Marxist tradition (however ambivalent) to emphasise that class should take precedence over national interests. By 1921 Soviet Russia had largely reconstituted the Russian empire, although without the countries to the west, including the Baltic republics of Estonia, Latvia and Lithuania, as well as Tuva in the east. The establishment of the USSR in December 1922 reflected a peculiar type of ethno-federalism, where the 'union republics' of Ukraine, Belorussia (as it was known before changing its name to Belarus in 1991), the Russian Soviet Federative Socialist Republic (RSFSR) and the Transcaucasian Federation (Armenia, Azerbaijan and Georgia) came together to form a new state whose legacy of dual federalism (with representation based on both territorial and ethno-federal principles) lives on to this day. A new constitution was adopted in January 1924 to regulate the new state structure. By the time the USSR disintegrated in 1991 the number of union republics had risen to fifteen.

Federalism was not, however, the preferred option for the Bolsheviks, since by definition it represents the constitutional entrenchment of the vertical separation of powers. Lenin also gave short shrift to the ideas of the Austrian Marxists Karl Renner and Otto Bauer, who favoured non-territorial cultural autonomy for minority national communities within the framework of a single state. Stalin, the long-time Bolshevik specialist on national affairs and Commissar of Nationalities, envisaged a unitary state with some autonomy for the regions and nationalities (the autonomisation plan). This would have made the regions units of a centralised Soviet state. Stalin insisted that minority peoples should not regress to a more backward system once they had become socialist. Hence, he argued, there was no need for the self-determination as earlier propounded by Lenin. The communist party itself was organised on unitary principles with its centre in Moscow and branches in the republics. Attempts by the Ukrainian Bolshevik party in 1920 to achieve some autonomy were suppressed by the Moscow leadership. In the event, Lenin rejected Stalin's autonomisation plan, alarmed by what he called 'Great Russian chauvinism' displayed by Stalin, Ordzhonikidze and Dzerzhinsky (none of whom was an ethnic Russian) towards the Georgian communists, and insisted on the association of formally equal nations in a federal system.

The guiding principle of Soviet federalism, as Stalin put it, was to be 'national in form but socialist in content'. The word 'union' (*soyuz*) in Russian denotes 'alliance', but the right to secede was only nominal. The long-term goal of Soviet communism was not merely to draw nations together but to bring about their merger. This distinction drawn by Lenin between 'drawing together' (*sblizhenie*) of nations and their 'merger' (*sliyanie*) was a crucial one for later developments. In the 1920s nationality politics were conducted in a relatively tolerant climate under the slogan of 'nativisation' (*korenizatsiya*). A Latinised alphabet was devised for the Turkic languages of Central Asia and Azerbaijan to replace the Arabic script, on the pattern adopted by Turkey itself. However, with the consolidation of Stalin's dominance, nationality policy took on a more chauvinistic and Russian face. The Turkic peoples were compelled to change their alphabet yet again and adopt the Cyrillic script. A peculiarly Stalinist cult of Russian glory was launched, and the historical and cultural traditions of minority peoples were undermined. Marxism–Leninism was combined with a Russianised version of Soviet communism to sustain a distinctive type of Soviet nationalism; but this was now, as we argued earlier, 'Soviet civilisation'. National cultures were reduced to folklore, and intellectual traditions that proved intractable were repressed. Nevertheless, as Terry Martin has demonstrated, the Soviet Union under Stalin remained an 'affirmative action empire', in which minority languages were preserved and national traditions preserved, as long as they adapted to the realities of Soviet power [111].

This applies equally to Russian identity as a whole. There were some who drew on the National Bolshevik ideas advanced by Nikolai Ustryalov, who in 1920 reversed the official slogan and argued that the new regime was 'socialist in form, nationalist in content', and praised the Soviet regime for having recreated the old Russian empire and restored Russia to great power status. The accord with Russian nationalism and the Russian Orthodox Church during the Second World War proved temporary, but it ensured the identification of Soviet power with Russian national interests for the duration of the emergency. Stalin's Russification policy was pursued not out of respect for Russian traditions but for perceived state interests. Soviet nationalism after 1945 certainly projected its Russian credentials, but at the same time forms of Russian patriotism that deviated from the Soviet path were persecuted no less than any other national deviancy – and in certain respects more, since the other major nationalities had their own republican party leaderships to shelter behind, whereas Russia lacked its own communist party and other attributes of statehood.

This problem became increasingly apparent in the post-Stalin era. By 1989 the 145 million ethnic Russians in the USSR represented 50.6 per cent of the Soviet population of 287 million, and the proportion was declining because of the marked tendency since 1960 for the birthrate among Russians to fall. Already in the 1960s the first springs of a revived Russian national consciousness emerged. The All-Russian Social Christian Union for the Liberation of the People (VSKhSON) talked of a uniquely Russian path, not democratic but benignly authoritarian, and endowed with a theocratic vision of Russian uniqueness. These themes were taken up by the journal *Veche*, edited by Vladimir Osipov, which between 1971 and 1974 proclaimed itself the voice of the 'loyal opposition'. It was characterised by a liberal nationalism that condemned 'the bureaucracy' and was concerned with regeneration based on Russian Orthodoxy and village traditions, and focused on Siberia as the rampart of a reborn nation from which the threats from China and the west could be rebuffed.

Solzhenitsyn was one of the first to emphasise the suffering that communism had imposed on Russia, and the enormous burden that it continued to place on the country. Solzhenitsyn argued that Russians should be permitted to pursue their destiny freed from the burden of empire. Liberal nationalists like him argued for the conversion of Russia from a military superpower to a spiritual great power, which they insisted would pose no threat to non-Russians or the outside world. Russian patriots of this sort were contemptuous of western liberalism but merciless in their condemnation of Soviet totalitarianism. The authoritarian implications of such views derive from their sense of moral absolutism; the attempt once again to remove politics from society and instead to impose an organic theocratic government of justice and order [163]. The development of a Russian national movement in the first instance was a cultural revival. The 'village school' of writers described the catastrophic effects of collectivisation on the Russian countryside while stressing the resilience of the Russian people. Vladimir Soloukhin, the author of *Vladimir Back Roads*, and Valentin Rasputin, who actively campaigned over ecological issues, above all to preserve the purity of Lake Baikal, the world's largest freshwater environmental treasure threatened by the building of a cellulose plant, and joined by the painter Il'ya Glazunov, criticised the over-rapid pace of industrialisation, which caused great damage to the environment and Russian village life.

Even in the heart of the CPSU a strain of communist Russian nationalism emerged, suggesting that Russia bore a disproportionate share of the burden of 'empire'. Conservative nationalists gathered around the *Molodaya Gvardiya* (*Young Guard*) publishing house of the Komsomol organisation and were apparently protected by Politburo member Dmitry Polyansky and allegedly by the KGB, since they served as a counterweight to unorthodox Russian nationalists, who focused on religious or human rights issues. It was for speaking out against conservative Russian nationalism that Alexander Yakovlev, then acting head of the Propaganda Department of the CPSU's Central Committee, was 'exiled' to Canada to serve as Soviet ambassador until recalled by Gorbachev. In a long article entitled 'Against Antihistoricism' in the 15 November 1972 issue of *Literaturnaya gazeta*, Yakovlev condemned the anti-Leninist stance adopted by nationalists and neo-Stalinists in some official publications, and denounced the awakening of Russian self-consciousness as 'patriarchal mentality, nationalism and chauvinism', for which he was never forgiven by the nationalists [21: *94–102*].

During perestroika the rivulets of a revived Russian national consciousness turned into a mighty river that breached the dam of Soviet power once it had gained the support of a renegade former communist leader, Yeltsin [41]. The numerous conservative nationalist 'historical–patriotic' groups such as *Pamyat* (Memory), *Otechestvo* (Fatherland) and *Spasenie* (Salvation) did not fare well at the ballot box. This rather undermined Alexander Yanov's view that the erosion of Marxist–Leninist ideology would not give way to the triumph of western rationalist or liberal ideas but would instead clear the space for the revenge of the nationalists. It certainly revived the Slavophile versus Westernisers debate of the nineteenth century over the role and path of Russian development. Yanov argued that a so-called 'Russian party', the fusion of unofficial and official Russian nationalism, would come together as the basis of an authoritarian but 'sanitised' (i.e., non-Marxist–Leninist) new ruling ideology [195].

While the Soviet state ensured Russian political pre-eminence, in economic terms Russia was far from being the most prosperous. Russian nationalists condemned the persecution of the Russian Orthodox Church, the excessive internationalism whose burden fell disproportionately on Russian shoulders, the distortion of Russian history, and the imposition of socialist realism in place of Russian romanticism [73]. National Bolshevism was condemned by more religious nationalists for espousing a Russian patriotism without a Christian foundation, based purely on the great power status of the Russian part of the Soviet Union – communism with a national face. Religious patriots stressed that Soviet nationalism was in fact antithetical to genuine Russian traditions; the Russian patriotism incorporated into Soviet nationalism, they insisted, served to buttress the power system but had little to do with genuine national traditions.

Stability and order in the communist revolution

Engels once remarked that 'A revolution is certainly the most authoritarian thing there is', and his observation certainly applied to Bolshevism in Russia. The communist order repudiated any authority outside the system itself. Thus Leninism gave rise to a solipsistic system in which its only reference point was the authority of the party; but the party, of course, was an abstraction, and real power was soon concentrated in the hands of a small group at its apex, who periodically entered into conflict with each other, in particular at times of leadership change. The absence of a legal mechanism rendered these times of succession ones of acute crisis, since not only was a leader being chosen but also the policy orientation.

The Bolsheviks after the October revolution were unable to establish a new political *order*, and hence were forced to maintain their rule by stability politics involving greater or lesser degrees of coercion. The distinction between *stability* and *order* is crucial here, applied to relations both within the regime and between the regime and society. Throughout their rule the Bolsheviks were concerned

with maintaining stability (and NEP was perhaps their most successful attempt), but order (*Ordnung*), the responsive relationship
between state and society reflecting the socio-economic and political realities of the time and the effective ordering of the state itself
giving birth to a new *Ordnungspolitik*, always eluded them. While
the English, American and French revolutions gave birth to new
political and social orders, typically through the mechanism of a
'restoration', the Russian revolution rejected the inherent order
of the society emerging out of a given stage of development, and
instead sought to establish an imposed order (a type of utopianism), which by definition displaced reality and whose strains generated the constant search for regime and social stability. According
to Trotsky [178: *273–9*], Stalinism was a permanent regime of crisis, but the Bolshevik *Ordnungpolitik* as a whole can be so characterised. Adaptation to society would mean the liquidation of the
communist order.

The struggle to maintain internal balance within the regime
and to retain its dominance over society entailed the enormous
exercise of techniques of 'manual control' over social and political
processes. This at times entered the mode of hypertrophy, as in the
1930s, and following Stalin's death in March 1953 his successors
were concerned that the machine did not run out of control again,
and thus threaten their own lives. This was the fine dividing line
that Khrushchev took in the destalinisation campaign: condemning the sins of his predecessor in his 'secret speech' in February
1956; but ensuring that the campaign did not escape regime control. Under the leadership of his successor, Brezhnev, this stifling
manual control was enough to maintain stability, through persist-
ent low-level police coercion against dissidents and others who
stepped out of line, but a functioning order once again eluded the
country as sources of renewal (above all through the adaptation
mechanism) were systematically stifled, giving rise to what later
was called *zastoi* (stagnation).

This is not to suggest that regime/society relations were based
on coercion alone, and at a certain level there were significant elements of consent [70]. The original revolutionaries were joined by
generations socialised into Soviet manners and mores, and for them
there was no alternative to the Soviet system. This was the beginning of a hybrid Soviet civilisation, fusing communism and Russia,
but there were two major limits to such a natural adaptation. The

first was the fear that a *political* adaptation would remove the raison d'être of the communist vanguard and their self-proclaimed goal of building socialism. This is one reason why those within the party who considered alternatives, as in the early Bolshevik years, were ruthlessly crushed. From a very early point stability-type politics and the associated coercion operated even, and possibly especially, *within* the communist party, suggesting that for the party leadership at least there was no prospect of a self-sustaining and non-coercive political order. When allied communist systems experimented with radical reform, as in Czechoslovakia in 1968, Warsaw Pact troops were sent in. The second inhibiting factor was *national*: adaptation of the communist regime to Russia, as began to happen after the war, would inevitably alienate the many other nationalities, notably the Ukrainians. The communist regime had to remain supranational, and to that degree imperial; but by the same token it hung disembodied over the society it professed to rule. This disembodied character of Soviet power became increasingly salient in its last years, and in every republic a process of national adaptation was underway, to a greater or lesser degree, by the late Brezhnev years. In Russia this was particularly problematic, since it was perceived in the other republics as a restoration of the Russian empire in a new guise.

The Soviet regime in Russia veered between two extremes: the frenzied campaigns of collectivisation, the great terror and the low-level purges after the war; and the periods of quiet that appeared to lack an intrinsic developmental dynamic and became increasingly involuted, losing revolutionary dynamism but trapped by the system's inability to adapt to the inherent realities of society. Only through the exertion of huge centralised mobilisation effort in various campaigns could specific results be achieved, as in the Virgin Lands Campaign of the 1950s that brought vast areas of Kazakhstan under the plough, the building of the Bratsk dams and associated power plant, or the Baikal–Amur Mainline (BAM) railway track, running to the north of the existing Trans-Siberian railway and designed to move this strategic line further from the Chinese border. The ultimate structural cause of the high level of coercion was the dissonance between patterns of subjectivity and the aims of the Bolshevik regime. Thus the 'stability regime' is not necessarily stable, and indeed the instability at the heart of the social order is its defining feature, veering from extremes of violence to periods of stability corroded by their inherent stagnation tendencies.

Leninism became an ideology of non-opposition, which was unable to integrate diversity as a feedback mechanism, and instead regarded every manifestation of difference as a challenge to the system. Civil society was driven down to the level of the family, and in ethnic, religious and other sub-political forms of solidarity. The Soviet system represented the apogee of hyper-governmentality, the attempt to govern and regulate ever smaller sectors of social existence. As we have seen, it was this pervasive regulatory urge that Kollontai condemned in her booklet of early 1921, *The Workers' Opposition*. The aspiration to hyper-governmentality penetrated society, and thus not even a socialist civil society was able to emerge, and instead a rather primitive form of community was imposed. This was mechanical community rather than an organic civil society, with stultified formal mechanisms of political and social participation. The denial of the opposition's intellectual arguments was accompanied by the denial of the right to exist. The aspiration for hyper-management, however, was not reflected in hyper-government. The USSR may well have been misgoverned, but it was also probably under-governed, an argument Arch Getty pursues in his analysis of Stalinism [56]. The problem was that no effective system of governance was achieved, and instead a much more primitive model of rule is probably applicable. Although Jerry Hough modified the title of Merle Fainsod's classic, *How Russia is Ruled*, to *How the Soviet Union is Governed*, there is much to recommend the former title.

It was precisely the inability to institutionalise civil society or to achieve a reciprocal order in intra-systemic relations that generated constant tensions and crises. The febrile intensity of political conflicts within the party, and at the same time their futility, reflected both the precarious basis of the regime and the nature of politics within it. The Bolsheviks had left the sphere of civil society in October 1917 and entered into a symbiotic and parasitical relationship with the state and with their own movement. They then drew up the ladder to deny other parties the opportunity to challenge for government by depoliticising society, and then proceeded to deal with civil society in various but always tutelary ways while at the same time ensuring that the relationship with its own movement, the rank and file communists and sympathetic 'non-party masses', was opaque and bureaucratised. The transparency in regime–society relations (in the sense that the elements of hegemony in authority relations were explicitly substantiated by coercion) was balanced by opacity in the workings of the 'black box' of Soviet decision-making, an opacity that was central to the regime of power from Lenin to Gorbachev.

4 The Great Retreat

Soviet civilisation represented a combination of Marxist–Leninist ideology and Russian realities, but, as we have seen, this 'civilisation' was deeply fragmented and no sustained synthesis created a fundamentally new reality with adequate social roots. Even though Russia was the heartland of the Soviet order, even here a gulf gradually widened between Soviet communist ideas and practices and an increasingly influential notion of 'Russia', existing apart and aside from the communist experiment; and indeed increasingly portrayed as much a victim of the communist experiment as, say, Estonia or Poland. As with the fall of communism in eastern Europe, discussion over the date when the Russian communist system moved into 'negative viability' continues. Some would start from the very beginning. Was it 1917, when Solzhenitsyn argued Soviet Russia set off on a futile attempt to build communism; was it Lenin's defeat of an independent workers' movement and opposition within the Bolshevik party, which stifled in perpetuity the sources of internal renewal; should the focus be on the alleged hijacking of the revolution by Stalin; or should we simply look at the exhaustion of the political and economic system in the post-war period? The debate continues, but we do know that from the 1970s economic indices turned sharply against the Soviet Union, despite its having achieved parity in strategic nuclear weapons with the USA in 1976. The downturn affected not only economic factors but also social ones. Above all, in the absence of systemic forms of renewal there were increasing symptoms of political breakdown, accompanied by the rise of corruption and the social degeneration of the elite that began to challenge the political viability of the system itself.

Modernisation and mis-modernisation

Although it is hard to credit today, Soviet Russia really did appear to offer a viable alternative to crisis-ridden western societies, in particular during the great depression from 1929. The intellectual atmosphere of the doom-laden 1930s is well captured by Richard Overy [123], with the Fabian Beatrice Webb condemning the irrationality and wastefulness of capitalism. The portrayal of the Soviet Union as a dynamic alternative was reflected in publications by H. G. Wells, but above all by the work of Sidney and Beatrice Webb, who in their book *The Soviet Union: A New Civilization?* in 1935 described the achievements of the system. Two years later, following the adoption of the 'Stalin' constitution in December 1936, they brought out a second edition, but the question mark was now dropped. They took the formal framework of government at face value, and thus failed to understand the real character of the system; and this at a time of mass terror [188]. Their work, and in particular the dropped question mark in the second edition, stands as an awful warning of the inadequacies of a purely legal–constitutional institutional approach to the study of government, giving rise in later years to the behavioural approach, focusing on how a system actually operates, which in turn was condemned for denigrating institutions; and, following a campaign to 'bring the state back in', gave rise to a 'new institutionalism' [145]. The Wellsian and Webbian approach (apologetics?) reached new heights with the book by Joseph E. Davies, the United States ambassador to the Soviet Union from 1936 to 1938 at the height of the purges. He commented that the Bukharin treason trial in early 1938 disclosed 'the outlines of a plot which came very near to being successful in bringing about the overthrow of this government' [35: *177*].

The Bolsheviks represented a combination of traditionalism and modernity. The attribution of guilt on the basis of class represented a return to ascriptive characterisations typical of traditional societies, but at the same time the rudiments of a modern society were built. The development of mass education was accompanied by the mass propagation of falsehoods. This was a type of modernisation from above, and was thus a forerunner of a distinctive genre that later encompassed Turkey, Egypt and some other countries. Modernisation was a term popular in the 1950s and 1960s to describe the process of rapid social change following decolonisation, and was used to evaluate the development of the west in comparison with its own past, and developing countries in comparison with western societies. Numerous models and phases of development were examined, and increasingly sophisticated typologies of modernisation and development were generated [43]. With the launching of the first sputnik in 1957, and the first man in space in April 1961 with Yuri Gagarin's circumvention of the earth, in response to which President John F. Kennedy launched the American manned moon programme, it looked as if the Soviet Union really was an effective alternative to western modernity.

By the late 1970s, however, the debate on modernisation had fallen into abeyance as the confidence in the western pattern of development was shaken by oil-shocks and stagflation, defeat in Vietnam and the palpable lack of political and economic modernisation, as earlier defined, in most of the Third World. Dictatorship, poverty, underdevelopment and the misapplication of science and aid seemed to be the hallmarks of the new age. Modernisation was condemned in the 1970s on the grounds that it suggested one path and one destination whereas in fact there might be a multiplicity of transitions and forms of political modernity. The latter assertion, however, has not been demonstrated, and indeed in all recent transitions different types of modernity appear only variations on a single theme.

It was in this spirit that Raymond Aron understood the USSR as a variant of progressive industrial society, and thus another version of the same social type found in western Europe [6: *42*]. By the late 1980s the language had changed and the USSR was now defined as a variant of modernity, albeit as incompletely modern, accompanied by a vigorous debate over convergence: the de-ideologisation of Soviet Russia complemented by an increasingly welfarist west. In the end, however, there was no convergence, and instead the Soviet-style alternative modernity collapsed. Thus the 1989 revolutions that put an end to the communist regimes in eastern Europe have been interpreted as a process of catching up or rectification [66; 5]. The view that the Bolshevik revolution put modernity on hold, however, is contested by Steve Smith on the basis of a comparative analysis of China and Russia, and instead he argues that 'communism, too, was a form of modernity' [160: *235*], accompanied by the development of individual subjectivity shaped by the great forces of modernity, such as nationalism, amidst the great collective identities imposed by the communist project.

The Soviet Academy of Sciences became the country's main centre of scientific research, continuing the tsarist model (based on the German system), which eschewed the Anglo-Saxon tradition of combining research and teaching in the universities. The Academy was not immune from Stalinist terror and underwent many reorganisations, but throughout the Academy offered a status to its members that transcended the regime and provided some protection for individuals and the autonomy of science [176]. Even in the harshest years of Stalin's terror bioscientists associated with the Academy were able to maintain a degree of professional integrity and to pursue lines of enquiry at odds with official policy [189]. It was out of this milieu that Andrei Sakharov emerged. Throughout his long years of travail and exile in Gorky, he was never expelled from the Academy, something that could only be done by a vote of the academicians themselves.

In civilisational and strategic terms the Soviet Union was indeed taking shape as an alternative, but the fundamental question is whether it enjoyed the structural properties of a viable modernity of its own, and here there remain some major questions. Olson has noted that in centrally planned economies 'The output of the economy is important not merely because it affects popular opinion, but even more because it is the source of the selective incentives that give the leadership of an autocratic society their power' [122: *18*]. His discussion of how societies increasingly suffer from 'institutional sclerosis' is certainly applicable to the Soviet Union [115]. In effect, he describes a process of 'systemic capture', in which groups leverage their position not only for personal advantage but to insulate themselves from the pressures coming from above. Soviet-type societies were increasingly unable to exploit the advantages of catch-up growth from the late 1960s:

> [O]ver time the small groups of administrators and planners in each industry or sector were able, by inconspicuous and subtle means, to overcome the difficulties of collective action enough to collude in their own interest, even though this reduced economic performance and thereby damaged the interests of the seemingly all-powerful Politburos above them. Over time a new class of subordinate officials came to enjoy spoils and powers that, in an early Stalinist phase, were possessed almost exclusively by the top leadership. [122: *20*]

A large literature from the 1950s began to describe the behavioural response of strategic groups to an environment dominated by the formal fulfilment of plan targets and formal obeisance to the political demands generated by the ideological system [13]. Already in 1980 Olson presciently warned:

> The economy that produces the selective incentives that persuade officials to carry out the orders of the government – the economy that pays the officials, the army, and the police – cannot continue indefinitely without substantial reform. Sooner or later middle level officials see the shrinking of the very output that is needed to reward them and this is demoralizing. When this occurs, it is no longer so clear that they have an incentive to carry out their orders and to protect the top leadership. [122: *21*]

By the late 1970s and 1980s it was clear that the USSR, despite Khrushchev's predictions to this effect at an agricultural conference in May 1957, would not 'catch up and overtake' the United States, but in practice was falling ever further behind. The prediction at the Twenty-First Party Congress in 1961 that communism, 'in the main', would be built by 1980 appeared increasingly unrealistic. '[T]he more thoughtful middle and upper levels in the Soviet Union', Olson noted, 'ultimately came to understand that the relative deterioration of their economy was no accident, but a result of the inherent contradictions of their economic system' [122: *22*].

Although formally Stalin modernised Russia, the nature of this 'modernisation' is highly questionable. Out of the Stalinist furnace a recognisably modern society emerged. A universal education system was established that at its best matched anything in the rest of the world, although in the villages, provincial towns and industrial areas the school system was subject to chronic overcrowding and lack of resources, features that persisted to the end. At the top, under Stalin whole branches of scientific enquiry and development were stifled: agronomy, biology, applied chemistry, linguistics, philosophy; and everywhere the lack of free exchange of ideas suffocated open-ended enquiry and discussion. The labour camp model was imposed on the Soviet search for the nuclear bomb, in a programme headed by the head of the secret police, Beria, and with scientists plucked from the labour camps and set to work in the *sharashki*, described so powerfully by Solzhenitsyn in *The First Circle*. Massive innovations in science and technology 'since the time of

Marx and Lenin cannot be readily exploited by Leninist-Stalinist institutions and ideas developed for an earlier age of steam, railroads and heavy steel' [49: *251*]. Among the many peculiarities of communist societies was the achievement of *individual* modernisation alongside archaic political relations and social development. Individual modernisation in this context suggests a person who is mentally open, cognitively flexible, and creative, with a definite sense of individual efficacy [75]. The model of social development was anachronistic and lacked the adaptive capacity to cope with new challenges.

Under Stalin and his successors the society and economy had become relatively developed, yet the whole pattern of Soviet industrialisation and modernisation was distorted. This was a type of *mis-modernisation*, which mimicked the developmental patterns of the advanced industrial societies but which lacked the fundamental dynamic elements that allowed those societies to develop. The concept of mis-modernisation does not suggest that there is only one true path of development; but it does argue that in the Soviet case the economic system became divorced from the needs of society and instead served an increasingly sybaritic elite. It became a self-perpetuating mechanism focused primarily on military–industrial tasks to enhance the international status of the ruling elite. The sacrifice of the consumer on the altar of industrial and military achievement, underinvestment in transport and other infrastructural networks, and the impoverishment of sectors serving social needs (such as health and education) left the country at best only partially modernised. A rudimentary universal system of primary and long-term health provision was created, but in a system that was starved of resources and that, after a golden age in the 1950s and 1960s, declined dramatically from the 1970s. The welfare system was crudely politicised under Stalin, with the disbursement of resources left to the trade unions in a system that excluded the great majority of peasants. Some of the great injustices were overcome by Stalin's successors, but once again the system was far from equal and universal.

Forced development inevitably took on anti-modern features. It is not surprising that one of the works that appears powerfully reminiscent of the Stalinist system is Karl Wittfogel's *Oriental Despotism* [192]. The Soviet political system represented the archaisation of political life, while its economy, so modern in form, reflected no less a Soviet primitivism about the elements that make up a modern dynamic economy. While the 'administrative-command system', as Soviet rule came to be known, was effective in achieving specific tasks such as industrialisation, collectivisation and winning the war, it was not so good at dealing with the consequences of its own modernising impulse. The Stalinist system undermined the bases of its own existence by acting as the midwife for an urbanised, educated and increasingly sophisticated society.

The party–state and citizenship

Under Khrushchev the system repudiated revolution from above, but although there were openings for greater participation this certainly did not endorse the idea of revolution from below. In the 1950s and early 1960s there were attempts to introduce forms of 'popular communism', notably the *druzhiny* (citizen patrols to keep order), but this reflected little more than an awareness that a highly bureaucratised social order generated alienation that could in due course turn into hostility. Even these limited initiatives were stultified under Brezhnev. Instead, the idea of 'developed socialism' of the late Soviet period offered civic peace in exchange for political passivity, accompanied by promises to improve standards of living and to allow people to get on with their private lives, as long as they conformed in public. The system practised a partial view of citizenship, limited to narrow forms of participation in public life. The period was marked by a crisis not only of communism but also of reform communism, already raising the question of whether the rather debilitated communism in Russia reflected a flaw in Marxism or in its implementation; whether it was a crisis of theory or of implementation.

Stalin laid a series of time bombs under the Soviet system. One with profound long-term consequences was the establishment of a pattern of patron–client relations to replace impersonal loyalty to the ideal. Loyalty to himself and the numerous little Stalins throughout the system set the stage for the degeneration of *nomenklatura* arrangements from a political system of appointments to a social caste. Soviet socialism in the post-Stalin era has been described as an 'administered society', in which terror and mass mobilisation gave way to routine and predictability [79]. Both

Stalinist mobilisation and Brezhnevite technocracy failed to fulfil the promise of commune democracy, developing the individual as an active and decisive citizen. Lenin had already reduced the scope for active citizenship, even of communist party members, and instead citizenship became an attribute of rote participation in formal Soviet participatory mechanisms, and lacked the crucial dimension of the development of human personality. Not surprisingly, the system bred cynicism and amorality in which altruistic civic engagement became increasingly rare.

The system was statist, but of a distinctive sort in which the state was unable to develop as an autonomous set of institutions but instead was colonised by the instruments of the party. The nature of the Soviet state remains ambiguous. As Rupnik noted: 'So if the party is not really a political party, the state is not actually a state' [148: *131–2*]. The communist party in the USSR indeed was not a classic party competing in the sphere of civil society for the votes of independent citizens, but instead was a permanent aggregative organisation to manage popular participation from above. As to the question of which social interests the state represented, the answer is fairly straightforward – its own and those of a politico-administrative neo-class, termed the bureaucracy or the 'new class' by Djilas [38]. Even the notion of 'bureaucracy' in the Soviet context is inadequate, because it was never a bureaucracy in the classic Weberian sense; and neither was it a class, because of its lack of social specificity. At the same time the political system failed to establish the autonomy of political institutions, that is, to build a modern state with a professional civil service and a differentiated structure of governance.

The party–state up to 1985 was able to insulate itself from social pressures and political demands from society. The Soviet party–state, fragmented and venal as it was, achieved a remarkable and well-nigh complete autonomy from society. This is not to say that social demands were not taken into account. There were feedback mechanisms, notably the institution of 'letters to the editor' whereby citizen concerns could be expressed, as long as they were couched in an ameliorative and not systemically critical manner. Worker protests in Novocherkassk in 1962 against a cut in wages and benefits were suppressed with loss of life by the army, but represented an early warning that administrative arbitrariness could threaten regime stability, to which the regime responded by monitoring social concerns. At times of elections citizens were also able to bargain about problems in exchange for their vote, and to that degree the ballot box did provide signals to the regime. Of course, elections were mainly a ritualised way of demonstrating loyalty and identifying the disloyal [198]. The bureaucratic management of society became increasingly sophisticated, leavened by a pervasive coercive capacity; but at the same time new social movements and aspirations began to take shape.

The absence of a genuine interactive democracy became a growing liability. While the notion of 'Soviet democracy' is not devoid of content, with high levels of public participation, certain feedback mechanisms and a developed network of representative institutions (notably trade unions, a national women's organisation, and various youth movements segmented by age), and a highly developed system of readers' letter, all of this was too often highly formalistic and bureaucratised. Above all, Soviet elections from the very first were less about popular preferences than a matter of mobilising support behind the regime. In the end, however, the absence of recognisably democratic procedures turned out to be not just an inadequacy of the system but *the* fundamental problem that determined everything else. One of the leaders of the humanist socialist movement in Yugoslavia in favour of the reform of communism, Svetozar Stojanovic, described the relationship between socialism and democracy as 'the epochal dilemma'. 'The growth of revolutionary dictatorship into socialist democracy,' he argued, 'is not simply one of the problems of socialism: it is *the problem of socialism*' [170: *108*]. This became evident in a series of mass uprisings in the post-Stalin era, which were essentially defensive and conservative in nature, usually responding in defence of local norms or in response to Khrushchev's ill-considered reforms.

The system disintegrated because of both its own contradictions and poor leadership in the post-Stalin years. As Remington put it:

> Thus the mobilization regime created a particular kind of 'dual society'. One society was the walled fortress of state power, with its official doctrine and its bureaucratic solidarity; the other was the 'little world' outside the state made up of individualised endeavor and reward, of small-scale production and trade, of hermetic pockets of unauthorized culture. Over the decades of Soviet rule, the more that the regime has sought to realize

its early dream of a fused and centralized authority stretching across state and society, the greater the bifurcation between the realm in which the state held sway and that of private action. When the regime has moderated its efforts at the mobilization of society, the fundamental diversity of the interests of its bureaucratic organs comes to the fore and defeats the leaders' hopes for coherent policymaking. [142: *21*]

In other words, without a permanent mobilisation effort the system would revert to the practices of the 'little world', undermining the authority and efficacy of state power. The development of a rich network of social self-help, called by Alena Ledeneva the 'economy of favours' (or *blat*), allowed individuals to overcome shortages and bureaucratic rigidities [101]. At the same time, Dmitrii Furman argues that the Soviet system appeared to do everything in its power precisely to undermine the ideological basis of the regime, making peace much more readily with various overtly anti-Marxist currents from the 1970s than with its own 'renegades', notably Trotsky and Bukharin [52: *9*].

For Marx, democracy was a social category rather than a political one. For Lenin, the war organisation of capitalism was in fact the embryo of socialism. In other words, rather than Soviet socialism focusing on the political emancipation of labour, it stressed the relations of production. As Lenin trenchantly put it during the democracy debate in 1920, 'Development is essential, democracy is dispensable'. However, the dialectic between development and democracy could not be reduced to such a crude formula, and in the end the absence of the pluralism that is an inalienable part of a genuine democracy stifled not only self-sustaining development but also the ability of the political system to renew itself in a timely manner. The Stalinist system was geared to war and struggle, but, as the external environment changed and more complex forms of interdependency emerged, the Soviet mobilisation effort looked not only increasingly absurd but also counterproductive. By 1980 over a fifth of Soviet GNP was devoted to military needs, an unprecedented level of militarisation in peacetime. The proclaimed raison d'être of the Stalinist-style mobilisation regime seemed increasingly anachronistic. Unable to generate a viable alternative modernity in which individual fulfilment could be combined with systemic dynamism, the Soviet system, quite simply, became pointless.

Sharman analyses 'the mismatch between an active, autonomous and powerful state, and a passive, dependent and weak society', which he considers a structural property of the system itself. This was 'dual Russia' with a vengeance, with the repressive state 'able to impose policy outcomes at variance with the preferences of the society it presides over, while maintaining its own political coherence and survival' [157: *14*]. The scope for adaptation was limited, and the system required ever greater efforts to achieve an ever-declining return. In such an arrangement, the stability politics of the Brezhnev era could not but promote stagnation. It was as if the battery were taken out of the clock, and the hands were turned manually; after a time, everyone would tire of the effort and let the clock stop. The search for stability was itself dysfunctional in a system designed to work through storming and campaigns. The attempt to maintain the stability of the system destroyed the sources of innovation and renovation, and there appeared to be no midpoint of order, no steady state of autochthonous development. After a long period of stagnation under Brezhnev, the next attempt at reform in the late 1980s soon moved beyond stability politics towards adaptation, but in the process brought down the system in its entirety.

Resistance and dissent

There had long been resistance to the constraints of Soviet thinking. These include the writings of Varlam Shalamov, the philosophical work of Merab Mamardashvili, the art of Il'ya Kabakov, and others who sought to overcome the consequences of the intellectual and physical terror experienced by Russian culture in the twentieth century [150]. The urge to resistance represented a basic challenge to both the theory and the practice of communist rule. It undermined the Leninist claim that the party knew best, and thus represented a theoretical challenge to the leading role of the party. It struck against Lenin's theory that the consciousness of individuals could be enduringly moulded by an external political agency. It challenged, moreover, the dirigisme on which party rule was based, the idea of a 'guided democracy' as the counterpart of the 'command economy' and 'administered society'. This growing societal resistance at first demanded little more than a relatively

103

circumscribed sphere of autonomy within the existing order, in which a degree of professional, moral and practical autonomy could be practised. One example of practical autonomy was the prevalence of joke-telling (*anekdoty*), mostly at the expense of the authorities, but which did not threaten the Soviet order [1]. Only later did the idea of independence take root, the aspiration to achieve areas of action in which an individual or a group was responsible only to themselves with the ability to interact with other groups and institutions on a contractual or equal basis. This represented the basis for a civil society but not yet at this point civil society itself.

The dissolution of communism in Russia began long before its actual collapse in 1991. In the post-Stalin years two main processes undermined the system from within. The first was social erosion, as the ruling class, formalised through the *nomenklatura* appointment system, degenerated into a venal and self-serving elite concerned with safeguarding its privileges. The network of special shops and agencies looking after their growing needs, first created by Lenin and much expanded by Stalin, now became a parallel society, insulating the elite from the hardships and shortages of daily life endured by the mass of the population. An acquisitive mentality seized the elite, and society as a whole became more oriented to consumerism. This was a struggle that the Soviet Union could not win, since in a battle over whether capitalism or communism could deliver the goods the former won hands down. The post-war years in western Europe had seen an unprecedented economic bounty that saw countries like Italy, which had been at roughly the same level of development as Poland in 1939, race into prosperity. The Soviet elite created its own islands of affluence, but the bureaucracy did not relax its exclusive claim to power. The concentration and unaccountable exercise of authority, which had always been the essence of Bolshevik rule, became increasingly intolerable, however, for a society that found itself condemned to second-rate services and goods, ruled by an increasingly incompetent and greedy elite.

The second process was connected with the first, namely the ideological erosion of the system. A common theme of this tendency was not only the loss of faith in linear interpretations of historical progress, but also an intense awareness of the costs that utopian projects for social and political amelioration impose on society. After 1968 the main tendency was the move away from attempts to reform the system (reform communism) and by 1988 the view that communist reform should be open-ended and adaptive became predominant – just at the moment when Gorbachev tried to apply a radical version of reform communism. The ontology in this period changed, with the old essentialist view of the working class giving way to more normative concerns. Social emancipation gave way to intellectual liberation.

The concept of resistance is usually associated with politicised forms of social opposition. In the USSR, however, resistance became a social phenomenon and took many forms. There is a fundamental distinction between resistance that in some ways entailed a conscious attempt to subvert the guiding principles of the system (independence), and resistance that entailed a spontaneous response to the operation of the system (autonomy). The elements of civil society survived in culture, the arts, sciences and humanities, and re-emerged through the political and subcultural processes of dissent. Above all, civil society was driven down to the level of the family, surviving in small ties of friendship and kinship. The two types of behaviour clearly overlapped but in the end represented two very different spheres. The resistance that considered the Soviet regime fundamentally illegitimate is very different from behaviour that took advantage of the porosity of the system to gain personal and group advantage or simply as a survival strategy.

The concept of independence fundamentally challenged the old way in which the communist system understood the relationship between the state and society. The independent movement represented a revolt of society against the tutelage of the state. This process is often conceived as a process of the reconstitution of civil society. Civil society at this stage certainly did not represent a sphere independent of the state, let alone being legally recognised and guaranteed by law, and even less was it based on private property and independent social organisations. A civil society is one in which rights are effectively guaranteed and in which interest groups can assert themselves. It goes without saying that such a pluralistic approach to society was a long way from being achieved in Soviet Russia before around 1987.

A line can be drawn from the various oppositions to the Bolshevik regime after October 1917, the intra-party oppositions of the early Soviet years, the inchoate but often heroic, although isolated, examples of resistance to Stalinism, the cultural opposition of

Khrushchev's thaw, the dissidents of the Brezhnev years, through to the rebirth of mass civic activism under Gorbachev. Often the oppositions were no more than losers in internal power struggles, and typically did not share even basic ideas, such as universal and equal citizenship under law, yet they represented the roots of intra-systemic pluralism. A certain level of resistance remained throughout the Soviet years, but its inability to take openly civic forms meant that when the lid was taken off opposition during perestroika it proved hard for civic associations and political parties to act as coherent aggregative mechanisms. There were thus four stages in the reconstitution of civil society. The first was the survival of the civic principle (*grazhdanskoe nachalo*) under Lenin and Stalin; the second the more formal emergence of organised opposition under Khrushchev and Brezhnev; the third was the establishment of legal security for a sphere independent of the state under Gorbachev; and the fourth stage was the accumulation of the full economic attributes and independence for civil society in post-communist Russia.

The Soviet system wilfully rejected precisely those elements that could have made it viable, and thus in the short term condemned itself to stagnation and in the long term to its own destruction. The failure to incorporate dissent intensified the blindness of a system based on authority rather than reflexive interaction with its own intellectuals, if not with society as a whole. There was a high degree of within-system dissatisfaction, especially among the rising generation, which did not take the form of overt dissent but which was not converted into an adaptive potential. Having broken a leg in 1969, for example, Boris Pankin (one of the Soviet Union's last foreign ministers) spent his convalescence reading the protocols of the party congresses. The inner story of the system created the first doubts in Pankin's mind, and he entered a period that he called 'legal dissidency', a frame of mind he claimed he shared with a generation of politicians, including Gorbachev and Shevardnadze, 'who made perestroika possible by changing the system from within' [65: 23].

Paul Hollander examines the internal dissolution of the system [71]. His focus is not on popular beliefs but on the way that important sections of the elite gradually became disillusioned with the communist system. Thus for him the fall was not just a matter of economic, political and social failures, but the erosion of belief in the system among the elite. This was accompanied, although not in every case, by the restoration of 'conscience', a category of human life that the Bolsheviks had as a matter of principle dismissed [16]. The Soviet system had been, in Aron's term, an 'ideocracy' legitimated by Marxist dogma, and with the dissolution of belief one of the fundamental props of the system was removed. The operating ideology required interaction with core beliefs to remain viable, and as the latter eroded the hollowness of the operating system became increasingly exposed. This was more than a gulf between theory and practice, although this was undoubtedly part of the story when faced by the grotesque privileges of the ruling elite while mass living standards declined, but growing doubts about the theory itself. The exercise of power without a transcendent purpose became increasingly tawdry, and this in turn exacerbated the venal degeneration of the elite itself. The core ideology in the past could always be used to justify the compromises and crimes of the operating system; but the operating ideology on its own was exposed as a mass of stale dogma and cruel practices. The internal dissolution prefigured the external collapse.

Dissent emerged out of the absence of democracy, defined not only in liberal democratic terms but also within the context of the concept of 'socialist legality' as developed by Khrushchev and his successors. At the Conference for Security and Co-operation in Europe (CSCE) in Helsinki in August 1975 the Soviet leadership signed up to the 'third basket', encompassing a range of human rights commitments. The legal dissenters thereafter were able to demand that the regime meet its own declared standards, let alone those of the west.

Roderic Pittey has identified two types of dissident. The destalinisation of the 1950s and the development of a repressive although increasingly porous system from the 1960s allowed a type of proto-civil society to emerge in the interstices of state power. Purges and generalised coercion were abandoned as instruments of rule and the imposition of social conformity was relaxed, allowing a space for a late Soviet public sphere to be created where some criticism of the system was allowed. Ideological discourse congealed into a performative ritual, and this retreat into hyper-formality created space for genuine debate, however tenuous and informal, which in the long run delegitimated the official sphere as the arena for the rote repetition of stale dogmas. While 'open dissidents' circulated *samizdat* and other underground publications and considered themselves in opposition to a system that they considered unreformable, 'inside dissidents' took advantage of the opportunities for greater debate within the system to advance various critiques and proposals for within-system reform [129]. The Institute of World Economy and International Relations (IMEMO) was established in 1956 and hosted a number of researchers who developed oblique critiques. Debate about the third world, for example, acted as a substitute for a critique of Soviet inequality and allowed critical analysis of the deficiencies of the communist order. Georgy Mirsky, an expert on the Middle East, was openly hostile to the invasion of Czechoslovakia in 1968 and later noted how the *embourgeoisement* of Soviet society 'Developed imperceptibly, masked by official phraseology' [129: *107*].

The 'open dissidents', however, were divided over the appropriate attitude to the system. People like Sergei Kovalëv, one of the earliest serious critics from the late 1960s, insisted on dialogue with the Soviet regime, arguing that the oppressive Soviet state should not be opposed by its violent rejection by the intellectual counter-elite. Kovalëv divided the human rights movement into two currents of thought: the legalists (*zakonniki*) and the politicals (*politiki*) [58: *31*]. He drew on the *Vekhi* collection to sustain his emerging defence of liberal human rights, in particular Bogdan Kistiakovsky's article 'In Defence of Law: The Intelligentsia and Legal Consciousness', and rejected the idea of the sovereignty of states when it came to human rights violations. As far as Kovalëv, and other leading oppositionists such as Larissa Bogoraz, were concerned, opening up dialogue with the regime meant an implicit acceptance that it had an evolutionary potential. This view was endorsed by Valery Chalidze, who as a matter of principle argued in favour of gradualism as opposed to revolution. Radical thinking had made the twentieth century so bloody, and instilled in him the normative view that working within the established laws of the state would achieve a more radical change than the pursuit of a counter-radicalism that entailed the danger of perpetuating in new forms the old closure. 'Certain basic axioms were clearly defined from the beginning of my involvement,' stressed Chalidze, 'the first being observance of existing laws but does not prevent my criticism of these laws nor disagreement with the official legal and ideological doctrine of communism' [27: *59*].

It has become a truism that in the Soviet Union everything was political except politics itself. Decisions were taken by a self-appointed group who claimed to know the laws of history and the correct decisions at any given time. The political system was effectively confined to a relatively small elite group, and the rest of society became passive consumers of their resolutions and the subjects of their campaigns. Specialist and professional groups could influence decisions at the margins and on certain issues, but this influence was not given political form, and the leadership was far from accountable to society. The quality of decisions in this closed system could not but be dysfunctional, especially with the absence of convincing feedback mechanisms and distorted information flows. It was clear that a significant part of the population resented their exclusion from effective politics, and were tired of being treated as children. More importantly, a number of Soviet leaders, including the new General Secretary of the CPSU, Mikhail Gorbachev, appointed in March 1985, also considered that 'we cannot go on living like this.' Now was his chance to try and find a better way.

Reform communism and dissolution

Although despotic in form, Soviet communism from the 1960s was not a classic tyranny, and certain features of what could have become a Soviet civilisation enjoyed a broad degree of passive popular support. The system did not fall because of the active hostility of the mass of the population, but because ultimately it proved unable to adapt to changed social and political demands in a way that could have organically integrated popular support into a dynamic political order. The exclusive claim to political sovereignty by the communist elite, as the sacred caste responsible for leading the people to communism, was unable to incorporate autonomous popular sovereignty and thus the system became ever more dogmatic and rigid, accompanied by the degeneration of ruling elites into a venal and self-serving group whose declarations about building communism sounded increasingly hollow, and ultimately risible. Once the people started laughing at the pretensions of the communist leaders, its days were numbered. The invasion of Afghanistan in December 1979, the rise of Solidarity in Poland in August 1980 and the death of the 'grey cardinal' of late

Brezhnevism, Mikhail Suslov, in March 1982 were all milestones in the fall of communism. In the final years of the Soviet Union both the structures and the ideology of the system atrophied. Unlike the Chinese Communist Party [156], the Soviet leaders were incapable of adapting to new challenges in an incremental manner, and instead the pressure for adaptation accumulated to such an extent that when change began it became a tidal wave of suppressed aspirations that in the end swept the whole system away.

Visiting Canada in May 1983, Gorbachev shared his concerns with the Soviet ambassador there, Yakovlev, who reports that they spent hours discussing the disasters awaiting the Soviet Union if nothing was done: 'The most important common understanding ... was the idea that we could not live this way anymore' [143: *294–5*]. Gorbachev believed that the old system remained viable but, like a powerful motor, it only required some fine tuning. Perestroika, he insisted, has 'been prompted by awareness that the potential of socialism has been underutilized' [61: *10*]. The remoralising strain in perestroika was crucial. Gorbachev noted that the decision to launch perestroika was prompted in part by 'our troubled conscience' [61: *25*]. Despite the revolutionary language, his was essentially a reformist programme, to save the system rather than to transform it. In the event, his tragic fate was to act as the destroyer rather than the builder; the more that he tinkered with the system, the deeper the crisis. The Soviet system turned out not to be a Mercedes Benz but a Trabant. Gorbachev's policies became increasingly radical, in part to stay ahead of his opponents. His reform communism only exacerbated the problems of what was already a system in crisis.

Revolutions tend to begin with a budget crisis, and the fall of the Soviet regime was no exception. Budgetary pressures were exacerbated by Gorbachev's spending spree in 1985–6, together with his anti-alcohol campaign, which deprived the state of one of its main sources of revenue. The January 1987 plenum of the Central Committee (CC) of the CPSU marked a step change in the development of a concept of reform communism, with discussions over *demokratizatsiya* (democratisation) and the call for the extension of competitive elections in the workplace, the soviets and the party itself. The local soviet elections of 1987, where some 5 per cent of seats were fought in multi-candidate contests, were the country's first competitive elections since the 1920s. In June 1987 a further plenum of the CC adopted a plan for the economic transformation of the country that gave greater autonomy for enterprises and increased rights for workers to elect their own managers. At the same time, *glasnost'* (openness) allowed some of the country's problems to be aired publicly. Gorbachev hoped that public debate would expose corruption and malfunctions. The relaxation of censorship gathered pace and by the end of perestroika in 1991 Russia had once again become 'the freest country in the world', accompanied by similar signs of the dissolution of order as had been witnessed in 1917. Rather than strengthening the system, the revelations only undermined the legitimacy of the regime as a whole.

Thousands of 'informal' movements were created dealing with social, environmental, gender and other issues, accompanied by the formation of the first political popular fronts and, later, parties. This was a type of negative popular mobilisation against the old regime, while the voice of supporters of the regime took an increasingly conservative tone. Reform communism was losing its natural supporters among the intelligentsia and national movements in the republic, leaving Gorbachev's perestroika increasingly exposed. The Nineteenth Party Conference (28 June – 1 July 1988) marked the transition to a period of genuine democratisation: although the CPSU was to retain a predominant role, it was now to guide rather than to lead. The overall aim was to create a 'socialist legal state', with the separation of powers and a revived legislature. In December 1988 constitutional reforms created a peculiar new type of parliament, a three-chamber Congress of People's Deputies (CPD), two chambers of which (the Soviet of the Union and the Soviet of Nationalities) were chosen in multi-candidate elections, while the third was made up of delegates from social organisations, including 100 guaranteed seats for the Communist Party. A similar model was later adopted for Russia, although without the delegated third chamber. The semi-free Soviet elections of March 1989 saw the defeat of many communist officials and the election by an overwhelming majority of Boris Yeltsin.

Democratisation in Russia began to outstrip what Gorbachev had intended for the USSR. The elections to the Russian parliament on 4 March 1990 were relatively more democratic (although by no means free) than the Soviet elections of 1989. In Russia democracy took the place of nationality politics as a mobilising force, and as mass electoral politics emerged Democratic Russia (*Demrossiya*), established in January 1990 to fight the March elections, came the closest to becoming a national movement. In May 1990 Yeltsin was elected chair of the Congress, and he used this position to advance an increasingly radical agenda of political and economic change. The adoption on 12 June 1990, by an overwhelming majority, of the Declaration of State Sovereignty of the RSFSR signalled the beginning of the end for the USSR. The Declaration stated that Russia is 'a sovereign state, created by historically united nations'; that 'RSFSR sovereignty is the unique and necessary condition for the existence of Russian statehood'; that 'the RSFSR retains for itself the right of free departure from the USSR'; and stressed the priority of the Russian constitution and laws over Soviet legislation [151: *466–8*]. The declaration of Russian sovereignty triggered an avalanche of sovereignty declarations – known as the 'parade of sovereignties' and the accompanying 'war of the laws'– which precipitated the disintegration of the Soviet Union.

The revolutions in the last months of 1989 swept away the communist regimes in Poland, East Germany, Czechoslovakia, Bulgaria and Romania. In Russia the tide of protest against elite privileges and popular shortages provoked a wave of protest, culminating in a demonstration half a million strong in Moscow on 4 February 1990 calling for multiparty democracy. With the people crying for freedom, the CC plenum on 5–7 February 1990 agreed to modify Article 6 of the 1977 Soviet constitution, guaranteeing the communist party's leading role, to remove the monopoly of the CPSU on political power. This was confirmed by the Third (emergency) meeting of the Soviet CPD on 14 March, which the next day strengthened Gorbachev's presidential powers. The abolition of the constitutional monopoly on power by the Communist Party in February 1990 brought an end to the era of one-party rule, which had in effect lasted since 1918. Free elections were introduced and the half-truths of *glasnost'* began to give way to genuine freedom of speech.

Gorbachev's concept of a 'revolution within the revolution' gutted the concept of revolution of all meaning; it also hollowed Soviet institutions of their inner logic and rendered them susceptible to even relatively light blows. Perestroika was imbued with the romantic mythology of revolution, but the ontological status of the concept is unclear. What sort of revolution would it be? It was clearly not class-based, unless we interpret perestroika as a revolution of the bureaucracy, allowing it to convert its privileges and property into power and ownership. Was it simply an elite revolution 'from above', but what was its ideology? Was it simply a programme of remodernisation, to return the Soviet Union to the main highway of civilisation? This was certainly an image prevalent during perestroika. In the event, this was a revolution with little vision of the future or even of a better contemporary political practice, but was permeated by a negative destructive logic. This was a revolution with revolutionary time in reverse. More profoundly, Gorbachev's achievement is best understood in the context of the subversion of the very concept of revolution, and he was therefore an inverted revolutionary. Gorbachev was more of a reformer than a revolutionary, however revolutionary the unintended consequences of his actions may have been. The rhetoric of a 'revolution within the revolution' became disengaged from political realities, the original reform coalition dissolved, and the programme of reform communism looked increasingly threadbare. Perestroika in the end played a negative role, a process that culminated in August 1991 when the old regime crumbled into dust. Once there was nothing left to destroy, perestroika came to an end.

Disintegration of the state

The fall of the socialist order, which we call the *dissolution* of communism, was accompanied by the *disintegration* of the Soviet state. These were two separate processes that in the end became mutually reinforcing. The federal structure of the USSR provided the 15 constituent republics with constitutions and governmental structures, and thus created the institutional resources for them to resist the assimilatory tendencies of the Soviet regime and then provided the framework for the disintegration of the regime itself [139, 24: *143*]. Ethnic affiliation was reinforced, and in some cases even created, by the Soviet system, despite its declarations in favour of class and internationalism. The Soviet Union fell victim to its own ideology, notably its belief that loyalty could be shifted to an abstract idea and its embodiment in the Soviet state rather than to any particular nation. To that degree the Soviet ideology was imperial, in that it emphasised supranational allegiance to the state rather than to any distinctive people. As the dissolution process accelerated in 1991 Russia hoped to leave the 'sixteenth republic' (that is, the empire of ideology and the communist party) while remaining united with the other fourteen, an exercise in geopolitical levitation that proved wholly unrealistic.

The Gorbachev reformist leadership, and later the Russian leadership headed by Yeltsin, to the end hoped that the dissolution of the communist system would not necessarily entail the disintegration of the Soviet Union, but neither could find a way of breaking the link between the two processes. Estonia led the way, with its parliament on 16 November 1988 declaring the republic's sovereignty, and Lithuania on 11 March 1990 declared its independence, followed by Georgia on 9 April 1991. Russia's declaration of state sovereignty of 12 June 1990 unwittingly proved the catalyst for a cascade of sovereignty declarations by union republics as well as autonomous republics, and in the end provoked the 'war of the laws' that culminated in the disintegration of the union and threatened the integrity of Russia itself. In declaring Russia's sovereignty its leaders were giving voice to suppressed national feelings, above all that Russia could and should be able to manage its own affairs (above all in economic matters) to a greater extent than hitherto, but only later did this take on overtly nationalistic forms. The Russian leadership at first simply wished to manage the territory called 'Russia', rather than assert that the country called 'Russia' should become independent or exercise tutelary leadership over the other republics in the union. As far as Russia's leaders of the time were concerned, there was nothing inevitable about the disintegration of the USSR.

Despite the generally peaceful character of the disintegration, Gorbachev did launch some punitive actions against the awakening nations, as in Tbilisi in April 1989, in Baku in January 1990, and in Lithuania and Latvia in January 1991. Against the background of an economic crisis and a growing wave of industrial unrest, together with Russia's support for the aspirations for sovereignty in the other republics, Gorbachev in spring 1991 decided that negotiation was the only alternative to war, defined by John Keegan as 'collective killing for a collective purpose'. Gorbachev tried to save the Soviet Union by renegotiating the terms of federation. In the referendum of 17 March 1991 71.3 per cent of the RSFSR's 79.4 million turnout (75.1 per cent of the total electorate) voted 'yes' to a renewed union. On 23 April 1991 in his Novo-Ogarëvo residence just outside Moscow Gorbachev signed with republican leaders an agreement that was intended to transform the USSR into a federation, the Union of Sovereign States. The 'nine-plus-one' agreement conceded greater power to the republics and agreed to an accelerated transition to the market economy. The new union treaty would be built from the bottom up, founded on the sovereignty of the republics and relegating Gorbachev and the central government to a secondary role. The new draft union treaty was revised on 23 July 1991 and was published on 15 August 1991, just five days before it was due to be signed by only three republics: Russia, Kazakhstan and Uzbekistan, itself a sign that the USSR was disintegrating. According to the draft treaty the USSR's strategic armed forces were to be retained under the union's operational control and the unified military–industrial complex was to be retained, although republics were to have their own national guards.

The creation of a separate Russian Communist Party in June 1990 reflected a conservative counter-mobilisation against the reform of communism, although it was not entirely opposed to reform communism. The dissolution of Gorbachev's definition of perestroika as a party-led programme of reform culminated in the coup of August 1991. A group of functionaries emerged, warning that Gorbachev's policies would lead to the betrayal of socialism and the destruction of the country. Conservatives argued that the union treaty would make the old structures of power redundant; it would certainly have put an end to their power. The growing democratic movement also now diverged from perestroika's reform communism and was united on the need to transform the old structures of Soviet power and to introduce the basic features of a modern democratic system. Within three days it was all over, and at a session of the Russian parliament on 23 August the CPSU was suspended in Russia, and Yeltsin ordered a number of communist newspapers to stop publication. On 24 August Gorbachev resigned as General Secretary of the CPSU and called for the dissolution of the Central Committee. On 29 August the USSR Supreme Soviet suspended the CPSU, and on 6 November 1991 Yeltsin banned the party in Russia. The attempt by conservatives to halt the dissolution by staging a coup only accelerated the demise of the old system and the state.

The idea of an independent Russia now triumphed, and step by step Russia took over the functions of the Soviet state. All the major

Soviet institutions were discredited, with the partial exception of the military and KGB, as the Soviet centre had in effect destroyed itself. The coup transformed the declarations of sovereignty of the republics into independence. The struggle between the declining USSR and the rising Russia was also a personal struggle between Gorbachev and Yeltsin, and between two principles of legitimacy. Yeltsin came to represent the aspirations of the Soviet republics for nationhood and democratic self-government, whereas Gorbachev was associated with the discredited idea of reform communism as well as the supranational idea of the Soviet Union. Russia took over all the remaining powers of the union, and at a meeting on 7–8 December 1991 in a hunting lodge in the Belovezhskaya Pushcha nature reserve in western Belarus the leaders of the three Slavic republics (Russia, Ukraine and Belarus) met to discuss the future. The Belovezh Accords declared that 'The USSR as a subject of international law and as a geopolitical entity has ceased to exist' and announced the formation of a Commonwealth of Independent States (CIS). Communism in Russia dissolved in August 1991, and in December the country in which it had been contained since 1922 disintegrated. At a stroke, Russia became not only post-communist but also post-Soviet.

The end of communism in Russia

While couched in a modern idiom, the legitimacy of Bolshevik rule derived from a metaphysical assertion that could only be sustained by the bullet and censorship and which, rather like tsarism, in the end did not prove amenable to evolutionary reform but ended in catastrophic breakdown. In the Soviet case this occurred in a time of peace and a relatively benign international environment. Despite attempts to broaden the Soviet regime's basis of legitimacy through the espousal of conservative Russian nationalism or the advocacy of welfare-state authoritarianism, the 'rule of the lie' could not coexist with truth, as the experience of *glasnost*' under Gorbachev so vividly demonstrated. Convinced communists like Yegor Ligachev, who endorsed a constrained type of reform communism, suffered genuine moral torment at seeing the achievements of 'socialist construction' being torn down in front of their eyes [104].

116

The Soviet Union was a super-ideological system, but the tension between its core and operating ideologies ultimately became unbridgeable. A deep gulf opened up between the system's 'core ideology', based in due course on the classics of Marxism–Leninism, and its 'operating ideology', based on the realities of power, society and the international system. For most of its existence Soviet politics was defined by an unstable dialectic between these two elements. This was vividly demonstrated by the two facets of the USSR's dual foreign policy: one pursued through the Comintern, advancing, at least at the rhetorical level, the international revolution; and the second, typically pragmatic, policy managed by the foreign ministry and foreign trade organisations. As John Dunn notes, 'from its very beginning Marxism has been profoundly evasive in its attitude to ... questions of strategic prudence' [42: *104*]. One of the fundamental features of the operating ideology was its monopolistic claim to be the only authoritative interpreter of the core ideology, even though the Soviet leader for eighteen years, Brezhnev, was never known to read a text by Lenin or Marx while General Secretary, and it is doubtful if he had done so earlier. It was this gulf, in part one between ends and means, that ultimately characterised the Soviet failure.

The operating ideology was taken in a new direction by Gorbachev, to the point that democratic socialism was placed on the agenda, but the core ideology remained a powerful force and could not simply be 'normalised' without provoking a fundamental crisis in the system as a whole, to which Gorbachev personally remained loyal. In other words, as long as reform communism remained limited to the operative ideology, it could not become hegemonic and part of the broader process of social and political renewal, and thus, like its previous forms under Brezhnev and Stalin (although with a profoundly renewed content), it remained locked in the same bind; but, once it shifted over to a programme of communist reform, then its adaptive capacity became potentially unlimited, even to the point of reforming itself out of existence – but by the same token it came into profound contradiction with the core ideology, generating tensions that proved incapable of resolution.

The Soviet party–state could adapt to society, but in doing so it stopped being the Soviet system. Its finest times were indeed war and the heroic period of War Communism and the first five-year plans; but stagnation was both cause and effect of its dissolution [cf. 191: *497*]. Gorbachev's project ultimately proved incompatible with anything approaching Marxism. At the Twenty-Seventh Party Congress in February 1986 he argued that it was time 'to overcome prejudices regarding *commodity-money* relations and under-estimation of these relations in planned economic guidance' [187: *504*]. Gorbachev sought to maintain the communist system without communist ideology, and at that point the system began to dissolve. It was unclear what would be the new rationale of rule. The alternative could have been some sort of de-ideologised union of republics, and there was a social basis for this. Alexei Yurchak argues that the fundamental values, ideals and realities of the communist order were genuinely important for many Soviet citizens, although they routinely transgressed and reinterpreted the norms and rules of the socialist state [196].

The Soviet regime eschewed legal–rational bases for authority, and the Bolsheviks' right to rule derived from a quasi-mystical assertion that they embodied the will of an abstraction, in this case the proletariat. The system from this perspective was unreformable, the product in its latter days of a decayed utopianism. The alternative to what was clearly becoming an unsustainable model of reform communism sought to move the terrain from utopianism to politics, from ontology to epistemology, and from ideology to reality. The old regime, committed to a 'revolutionary' model of reform communism, could not make that transition, and it was left to the new forces to do so. Gramsci argued that the old regime in Russia had lacked depth: that the facade of state power was not supported by flowing ramparts of civil society. The same could be said of the Soviet regime in 1991. Once the institutions of the party–state were abolished there were no elements of a systemic order ready to sustain the system. As Zdenek Matejka, one-time Secretary General of the Political Consultative Committee of the Warsaw Pact, put it with reference to plans to restructure the organisation: 'What started as perestroika, ended with complete dismantling. The same happened with the Soviet Union and with Communism itself. Such an outcome was inevitable and perhaps would be the same whenever some new Gorbachev tried to start reforming something unreformable. He could be reasonably sure he would also end up with the total destruction of what he had set out to reform.' [112: *64*]

Although Gorbachev remained loyal to a socialist vision, this was no longer based on a revolutionary transformative agenda. He did not simply adopt a pragmatic technocratic approach – the system might have survived if he had – but his commitment to the traditional logic of the emancipatory revolution was accompanied by the abandonment of traditional means, an unstable mix whose contradictions became increasingly evident with each passing year of perestroika. The removal of the rationale for the external Cold War, moreover, undermined the logic for internal mobilisation [15]. As with Dubček earlier, 'What he [Gorbachev] and other reformers of similar disposition ... did not seem to realize was that reforms carried forward beyond a certain point would undermine the very foundations of the political order that they sought to preserve' [71: *193*].

Few empires have collapsed with so little bloodshed and so few international convulsions, unprompted by failure in world war or the pressure of barbarians at the gates. Andrei Amalrik in 1970 predicted the fall of the Soviet Union, although his emphasis on the Chinese threat appears misplaced, but in the end his view on the disintegration of the 'empire' was prescient: 'Just as the adoption of Christianity extended the life of the Roman Empire for 300 years, so did the adoption of communism extend the Russian empire for several decades' [2]. The retreat of the communist empire from eastern Europe was relatively unproblematic, since the dissolution of communism represented the removal of the shackles of an ideology and power system imposed by arms from abroad. The fundamental question is whether the system was indeed an empire, and, if so, of what type. Solzhenitsyn argued that the Soviet Union was not a *Russian* but a *communist* empire, especially in the light of the fact that Russians did not enjoy any special privileges in the system [165]. The Russians were certainly identified with the dominant ruling group, but this was not so much a derivative of their ethnic pre-eminence as their positional advantage as loyal servants of the system. Beissinger stresses that an empire is less a structure than a set of practices with which its constituent peoples identify as 'ours' or 'theirs' in different measure as the perception of interests and balance of advantage changes over time [11]. By the late 1980s the balance had shifted radically, and even the Russians, as prefigured by Solzhenitsyn's argument, began to perceive the 'empire' as alien and oppressive.

The revolutions of 1989–91 were perhaps the most significant events of the century: it is the nature of their significance
that is contested, above all focused on what sort of societies they
were revolting against. The Soviet Union represented an empire
without a core; after 1985 it also became one without a cause as
Gorbachev systematically stripped the system of its ideological
rationale. Even before this it was clear that Soviet obeisance to
the idea of world revolution had become mere lip service. As the
veteran Soviet diplomat Oleg Troyanovsky put it, 'Early on, the
idea was that the world revolution was just outside the door. But,
little by little, it became a more or less theoretical thing, just like
the second coming of Christ. You preach it, you are supposed to
believe in it but no one takes it seriously' [179]. The erosion of
ideological fire was accompanied by the realisation that the Soviet
Union was a one-dimensional superpower, with a military capacity
far in excess of what its economy or society could bear. Party bosses
were trained to apply their energies downwards, to suppress dissent
and to ensure social order, but were unable to generate a developmental dynamic. Under Gorbachev they suddenly found that the
challenge came from above, to interpret the various mixed signals
and exhortations for change in unexpected and unclear directions.
There were no structures or preparations to achieve this.

The fall came about as a result of the interaction of systemic
problems with personal interventions [172]. The structural problems were legion, including declining economic efficacy, the
weakening of central authority that in some ethno-federal union
republics took the form of effective separatism, and a variety of
social problems. However, the emergence of an agent, Gorbachev,
who reshaped political institutions but in tackling the power of the
apparat and allied institutions undermined governmental efficacy
in its entirety, was crucial in transforming crisis tendencies into
a full-blown crisis of state viability. Numerous internal political
and institutional rifts emerged, notably between advocates of ever
faster reform and those who favoured a more moderate pace, and
between the military and the KGB. Commenting on this, Suraska
notes that the Soviet Union would have been able to maintain
its superpower status if Gorbachev had not intervened in such a
devastating manner [172: 2 and *passim*].

The 1989–91 fall of communism was as much a cultural or civilisational collapse as a more narrowly political or economic one.

The whole nexus of ideas, political practices and elite preferences moved in different directions, and the Soviet way of life could no longer be sustained. The old regime had stopped being the old regime in most essentials before it fell. Reform became the executioner of the system. The dissolution of communist power was not so much a democratic anti-communist revolution as the collapse of an exhausted system, accompanied by the redistribution of power between sections of the old elite. In Russia the democratic revolution proved to have a very fragile base.

Perestroika clearly illustrated that the system did not lack the capacity to reform itself; but it no less clearly demonstrated the historical trap in which reform of Soviet-type communism found itself – once started, reform would not save the system but destroy it. For many this ontological dead end derived from the fundamental character of the revolution that had created the system in the first place, imposed upon a society and ruling through varying but always high levels of coercion thereafter. There was no mechanism to shift from a stability system to a system based on order, and thus no ability to institutionalise accountable political power in an adaptive process. Reform communism, a programme that had been on the agenda since at least the death of Stalin, proved unable to convert the system from stability to order. Jakub Karpinski sums it up as: 'no coercion, no communism' [78: 7]. If Koestler was right and Stalin's destruction of the old Bolsheviks represented the logical triumph of Bolshevism over itself, then one would have to accept the logical corollary and accept that 'Bolshevism did not contain a democratic alternative and therefore that hard-line anticommunists were right to deny the possibility of a peaceful evolution of the Soviet regime of a genuine socialist democracy' [187: 459].

There are echoes of these sentiments in Vladimir Putin's *Russia at the Turn of the Millennium* of December 1999, when he argued:

> For most of the twentieth century, Russia lived under the communist doctrine. It would be a mistake not to recognize the unquestionable achievements of those times. But it would be an even bigger mistake not to realize the outrageous price our country and its people had to pay for that social experiment.
>
> What is more, it would be a mistake not to understand its historic futility. Communism and the power of the Soviets did not make Russia a prosperous country with a dynamically developing society and free

people. Communism vividly demonstrated its inability to foster sound self-development, dooming our country to lagging steadily behind economically advanced countries. It was a blind alley, far away from the mainstream of civilization. [136: *212*]

While many retained a belief that communism had been a noble ideal poorly implemented, others argued that the ideal had been the root cause of the misery inflicted upon Russia. This, for example, was the view of Aleksandr Tsipko, a member of the Central Committee apparatus, who in 1988–9 published a devastating critique of Marxist ideas; powerful not for what he said but for the intense effect they had on a society which had been shielded from genuine discussion about the ideological precepts of the system for so long. Both Lenin and Stalin believed in the power of ideas, and for this reason made sure that they controlled availability to the public. Tsipko argued that Marxism had to be cleansed 'of certain typical blunders of nineteenth century thought' [180]. Amongst these 'blunders' was the attitude to the state, although Marx's thought in this respect was not typical of nineteenth-century thinking. The common refrain at this time was that Marxism–Leninism had no potential for development, and that the 'socialism versus capitalism debate had outlived its times'. A range of ideas were advanced by reform communists and neo-socialists, who argued for a far less state-centred form of socialism and certainly not a Leninist party-based form.

It is in this context that the argument has been made that perestroika could not be anything but a failure because there was no historical space into which it could move. Already Alain Besançon [14] had noted: 'If the absence of socialism is caused not by technical but by ontological reasons, if it does not exist simply because it cannot exist, then its introduction will lead only to the destruction of what already does exist.' In a similar vein, back in the 1970s Gyorgy Bence and Janos Kis (writing under the pseudonym of Marc Rakovski) [138] argued that original categories were required to study Soviet-type systems, which were *sui generis* new social formations embarked on a journey up a historical dead end with minimal internal potential for further development. Rather more poetically, Solzhenitsyn argued that the Soviet system represented a mad dash down a blind alley. In the same vein, the Democratic Union (the first independent political party in Russia since the revolution) from 1988 advanced the view that the Soviet Union was intrinsically totalitarian and represented the 'Asiatic mode of production', a 'dead end of historical development' that had begun in 1917.

The banners carried by some of the half a million demonstrators on 4 February 1990 calling for the removal of Article 6 of the 1977 Soviet Constitution stated '72 years on the road to nowhere', and reflected a popular view that the Bolsheviks had led the country onto a barren path of social development. The August 1991 events in a structural sense represented an attempt to find a way out of this political stalemate, as well as out of what was perceived to be the broader dead end of history, not only of Gorbachev's reforms but also of the whole epoch of Bolshevik power [109].

5 Communism in Russia

The Russian revolution in 1917 promised freedom, yet the revolution as a form of collective political action removed restraints on the exercise of power, and prepared the way for a greater despotism. The Bolshevik regime operated within the parameters of a revolutionary socialist ideology with a very strong Enlightenment perspective of progress, deculturation and denationalisation. Walicki has convincingly argued that the Bolshevik revolution remained remarkably loyal to the basic Marxist vision of the destruction of commodity production [187]. Even Stalin in his own way was guided by his interpretation of the Marxist classics and did not simply use ideology as a philosophical camouflage to disguise his undoubted striving to gain and maintain power [184]. In the end the USSR represented a transient challenge. We now know that Bolshevik practices largely vitiated any 'progress' that may have been achieved, not only in the sense that the price in human lives and suffering was enormous, but that the very structures that the Bolsheviks built, in the economy, society and the polity, proved unsustainable. The Bolshevik regime solved none of the most urgent tasks facing Russia – not the national question, economic development or political coherence. More than this, communism was unable to maintain the unity of the territorial formation that had been created over the course of nearly a millennium. The Bolsheviks had recreated a state covering the old tsarist territory by the early 1920s, but once again in the early 1990s the territory fell apart. The Russian communist challenge to western modernity, moreover, was unable to establish a viable, let alone a convincing, alternative social order. The picture, however, is not one of unmitigated failure, and we need to examine the various levels of achievement. The history of communism in Russia remains highly politicised, and to that degree it remains part of the living fabric of contemporary political development.

The great experiment

The French revolution had provided Hegel with the example *par excellence* of the 'disaster that must follow any attempt to establish a state on the basis of abstract rational principles, unaccompanied by the development of an appropriate subjective consciousness on the part of its subjects' [98: *2*]. Karl Korsch argued that subjectivity lay at the heart of revolutionary action, while Gramsci, too, stressed that revolutionary transformation was more than the capture of state power but entailed the replacement of one hegemonic order by another. Emile Durkheim had consistently warned against 'simplistic revolutionism', arguing that political and legal changes are determined by the whole structure of society [53: *1*]. Although the Bolshevik revolution at first attracted Durkheim and his associate, Marcel Mauss, because of its appeal to a type of social solidarity based on corporate representation, their long-standing critique of Marxism was soon justified: '[T]he Marxists lacked any sophisticated understanding of the necessary structures of the social division of powers in a socialist state' [53: *5*]. For Durkheim, revolutions could not create a new order at a single stroke and destroyed more than they created; and in the Russian context this was exacerbated by what he considered to be Russia's 'fundamentally mechanical' society in which the organic division of labour had barely developed and instead society was characterised by its 'segmental structure' [53: *159*]. The Bolsheviks swiftly destroyed the intermediate collectives that were so important for Durkheim, and instead established a military-style economic society that by the end, paradoxically, was devoured by the military–industrial complex that it fostered.

Frederick Engels wrote to his Russian friend Vera Zasulich on 23 April 1885: 'People who boasted that they had made a revolution have always seen the next day that they had no idea what they were doing, that the revolution made did not in the least resemble the one they would have liked to have made' [33: *101*]. This is indeed the case, but certain actions have predictable consequences. Bakunin had warned what might happen if intellectuals came to power: 'Woe to mankind if thought ever became the source and sole guide of life, if science and learning began to govern society. Life would dry up, and human society would be turned into a dumb and servile herd. The government of life by science could have no other result than to turn all mankind into fools' [8: *135*].

Mauss's exploration of the character of Bolshevism confirms this prediction. He raised the question of whether the Bolshevik experiment proved or disproved socialism. Despite Bolshevism having gained authority from the fact of victory, it remained, in Mauss's view, 'an experiment in the vulgar sense of the word, a try-out' [113: *167*]. Despite the 'indisputable grandeur' of the Bolshevik experiment, it repudiated what had been central to the west European revolutionary tradition, namely the democratic, republican and legalist elements [113: *168*]. He noted the combination of 'ferocious dogmatism' and 'versatility undaunted by any contradiction' [113: *174*], the tension between the core and the operating ideology which at times became a yawning gulf. The maximalist doctrine of the Bolsheviks freed the movement of scruples, and allowed a small group to seize power, but by the early 1920s the gulf between the regime and society was clear: 'Apathy on the one hand, clear, fanatical will and power on the other, that is the relationship which then and now unites the Russian people and its Bolshevik despots. ... Bolshevism is grafted onto Russian life, onto the Russian Revolution which it will soon have controlled for six years'.

Contrary to interpretations, advanced in particular by Trotsky, that the Bolsheviks were forced to drastic measures because of the intractable character of Russian backwardness, Mauss argued that in fact the Bolsheviks from the first were parasitic on the Russian revolution: 'They exploit the Russian Revolution, its ideology, or rather they manipulate Russia, its human material, its disproportionate wealth in men and materials' [113: *178*]. Violence had been inherent in the Bolshevik programme, and thus massive extra-legal coercion was not an improvisation in the face of circumstances but generated the circumstances in which such violence was perceived as necessary. For Mauss the conclusion was clear: '[T]he Russian Communist experiment will have served at least one purpose – to teach nations who want to reform how they should go about it and how they should not go about it. They must retain the market and money; they must develop all possible collective institutions; they must avoid incompatibilities between free associations and collectivism, and between the right of association, including the right of the majority, and individualism' [113: *203*]. His conclusion was that 'The Russian events neither confirm nor contradict socialism' [113: *204*] since they had little to do with socialism, a view that

Kautsky had earlier adumbrated, to Lenin's intense annoyance, and a judgment that stands the test of time to this day.

In 1917, to use Aron's formulation, the state was conquered through society, but society was unable to sustain its independent political subjectivity and the problem that Marx wrote about so eloquently in his *The Civil War in France*, of the state as an 'excrescence' of alienated social power, returned with redoubled force. The Soviet Union was a system of power rather than order, failing to establish an *Ordnungspolitik* in which society was organically integrated into the working of the state system. Instead, social organisations acted, in Lenin's memorable words, as 'transmission belts' for party influence. This inhibited the development of more hegemonic types of rule, of the sort that had begun to take shape before 1914, and the system remained not only deeply coercive but intensely administrative, and in its last period even the shift to more technocratic modes of rule was accompanied by the continued rote imposition of an increasingly meaningless ideology. Intense politicisation was not accompanied by an autonomous level of 'the political', an arena of choice and formalised contestation. Gorbachev's reform communism, initially at least, sought not to depoliticise the system but to repoliticise it in new ways, and Russian politics to this day remains stamped by the failure of an autonomous political arena to sustain itself.

The Soviet experiment in Russia indicates the truth of Walter Benjamin's remark that [communist] revolution was not a runaway train but the application of the emergency brake. The communist project hoped to create a sphere of stability in the ceaseless anarchy and dynamism of capitalist modernity. Communism in Russia achieved this with a vengeance in the post-Stalin era, taking the form of a stability system that represented not just the manual management of social processes but also the deeper repudiation of the restless innovations of capitalist democracy. This feature endows Brezhnevite stability with attractive qualities that remain a subject of nostalgia even for a younger generation in post-communist Russia who never enjoyed its benefits. Late communism was a profoundly conservative system, which in the end was unable to find a way to combine stability with self-perpetuating order.

Furet makes a devastating critique of the communist experiment, stressing its utter lack of any contribution to human development: 'All that remains of the regimes born of October is what they sought to destroy' [51: *vii*], namely bourgeois democracy and capitalist markets. He stresses the point that 'The only thing to be found among the debris of Communist regimes was the familiar repertory of liberal democracy' [51: *ix*]. While the French revolution and the Napoleonic era laid the foundations of a state that has lasted centuries, the Russian revolution dissolved to leave no legacy: 'The October Revolution ended not by being defeated in war but by liquidating all that it had created. When the Soviet empire fell apart, it was in the strange position of having been a superpower without incarnating a civilization' [51: *viii*]. On this point there is disagreement, since Stalinism has been described as a civilisation [94] and the whole Soviet era has been described as such by Andrei Sinyavsky in his *Soviet Civilization: A Cultural History* (1990), and Alexander Zinoviev in his powerful description of the reality of Soviet life in *The Yawning Heights* and *The Radiant Future*. Furet's point is a fair one, since he is not arguing that while it existed the Soviet Union did not act as an entire system of values and practices; but his focus is on what was left after its dissolution – which in his view is nothing.

He saw communism in Russia as the constant feeding of an illusion, which he defines as the need for the system to conform to 'the necessary development of historical Reason, and that the "dictatorship of the proletariat" thus appeared to have a scientific function'. This was more than 'an error of judgment, which, with the aid of experience, can be discovered, appraised, and corrected, the Communist illusion involved a psychological investment, somewhat like a religious faith even though its object was historical' [51: *ix*]. Thus the illusion was not attendant upon communism but its very foundation. It drew on 'the political imagination of modern humankind', but it could only survive 'by constantly adjusting to circumstances', with the unanticipated being integrated into the belief system and thus 'History was its daily bread', and the system collapsed when it stopped being fed. The core of communism was its belief 'in salvation through history' [51: *vix*], and it died when this vision was finally repudiated. Communism represented a 'closed circuit of the modern political imagination' [51: *x*], and when this was finally broken open there remained no historical terrain in which the system could survive, let alone flourish. Thus the answer to the question of what communism could have become is clear: 'today, Communism is completely contained within its past' [51: *x*].

While Furet provides a powerful refutation of communism's practices and its ideological closure, Hayek seeks to demonstrate its logical incoherence. He argues that civilisation depends on 'the extended order of human cooperation', or, in short, capitalism. This emerges not from human design or intention but spontaneously, based on certain moral practices whether humans like these practices or not, notably the 'comparative increase of population and wealth'. If the socialist alternative of non-market-based solutions actually worked, then capitalism would face a real challenge, but Hayek's argument is that 'there is no known way, other than by the distribution of products in a competitive market, to inform individuals in what direction their several efforts must aim so as to contribute as much as possible to the total product' [69: 6]. Thus the rationality that lies at the basis of communist claims in his view is irrational, since it lacks foundation in the spontaneously generated moral precepts that underpin an 'extended order', and thus can deliver neither social justice nor economic efficacy. While easily criticised for their inability to generate a critique of the inadequacies of evolutionary market mechanisms, the potency of Hayek's arguments when it comes to the experience of communism in Russia cannot be denied. Alec Nove [120] had indeed come to a similar conclusion in examining the 'economics of feasible socialism', based on Soviet experience. He described not only the economic dysfunctionality of the planned economy (although it was based less on planning than on commands), but also the political consequences of the abolition of the market, in particular the need for a centralised system that would inherently tend to the despotic. A more detailed macroeconomic analysis of the systemic failings of Soviet-type economies is provided by János Kornai [91].

Marxists, of course, take a very different view. There are at least three major families of theories trying to explain the nature of Soviet communism. The first is the 'state capitalist' school, advanced by Max Horkheimer, Tony Cliff, Cornelius Castoriadis and many others, arguing that formal socialised ownership over the means of production disguised the power exerted by ruling elites over the appropriation and distribution of surplus value, and thus the proletarian character of the revolution gave way to bureaucratic consolidation. The second perspective developed Trotsky's idea that the Soviet Union was a 'degenerated workers' state', which assumed that at some point the Soviet Union had been a genuine workers' state (usually considered to be the period when Trotsky was in power), and had then degenerated when Stalin became predominant. A workers' state is defined as one in which the proletariat predominates in a system that has abolished the private ownership of the means of mass production. The demonisation of opponents had begun from the first days of the revolution, and the intraparty opposition led by Trotsky in the 1920s was cut from much the same cloth as Stalin [68]. A third view argues that the Soviet Union had devised a completely 'new mode of production', combining a hybrid post-capitalist economic formation with a political system combining bureaucratic and worker power [183]. The intensity of the historical debate disguises its somewhat scholastic character. These discussions had a certain resonance when the prospect of a socialist revolution in the west retained some credibility, but with the waning of the era of socialist revolution what had once been passionate differences over points of Marxist interpretation joined the same dustbin of history as Soviet communism itself.

All perspectives on communism on Russia viewed from the experience of the collapse will inevitably be misleading. By reading history backwards they impute an inevitability to events that might not inherently have led to that particular outcome. This is the view of Claude Lefort, who takes issue with the argument that the anti-modern and undemocratic aspects of Soviet communism inevitably led to collapse. Bolshevism in power represented a permanent civil war, and thus was not only transformative of socio-economic structures but entailed the fundamental reconfiguration of socio-cultural relations, in which the party was both embedded in society and apart from it. This was not a system of autocratic power of the traditional sort but represented a type of 'popular' democracy in which the party was both ubiquitous and all-pervasive, but by the same token hard to localise [102]. It is this disjuncture between the universality of the communist party and its disincorporation from society that in the end became a gulf that no amount of 'reform communism' could bridge.

Anticipating and interpreting the end

The alleged failure of Sovietology to predict the Soviet collapse is a largely meaningless exercise [cf. 30]. We can distinguish between *prediction*, the statement of some future event at a more or less specified time precluding other potential outcomes, and *anticipation*, suggesting the possibility of a variety of outcomes with an open-ended time frame. A vast body of literature and academic writing from the very first days of Bolshevik power had *anticipated* the inherent lack of viability of a post-market stability regime, and detailed the enormously disruptive political and social consequences of the project. In this connection we need only cite Andrei Platonov's writings of the early Bolshevik period (especially *Kotlovan* and *Chevengur*) and Yevgeny Zamyatin's dystopian *We*, completed in 1921, the precursor of a distinctive twentieth-century genre. Zamyatin's community (called the United State) was based on the proposition that freedom and happiness are incompatible, and already in 1920 he noted that 'elections themselves have rather a symbolic meaning. They remind us that we are a united, powerful organism of millions of cells' in which there was 'no place for contingencies', like not knowing in advance the result of the elections [197: *129*]. On the academic front, Bertrand Russell's *The Practice and Theory of Bolshevism*, a devastating critique of Bolshevik rule, was first published in November 1920. The moral collapse associated with the rise of Bolshevism was explored, among others, by Berdyaev, while G. P. Fedotov fruitfully explored the tension in the relationship between Russia and the west. We have noted Mauss's scholarly evaluation of Bolshevik power.

In his justly renowned 'Mr X' article of 1947, George Kennan noted that 'Soviet power, like the capitalist world of its conception, bears within it the seeds of its own decay.' He presciently warned that if 'anything were ever to disrupt the unity and the efficacy of the party as a political instrument, Soviet Russia might be changed overnight from one of the strongest to one of the weakest and most pitiable of national societies' [83: *580*], an insight whose implications Gorbachev might well have considered with profit. In a similar vein, Fehér et al. already in 1983 had noted of Soviet-type systems that 'The whole vast apparatus of domination which seemed omnipotent and omnipresent the day before, disintegrates the next day' [46: *21*]. The stability regime itself eroded the bases on which a functioning political order could be built, and the manner of its collapse was immanent to the system itself. The fall of the regime in 1991 added little that was not already well known; but the timing and character of the collapse was something that simply could not be predicted. While the factors conditioning the fall of the Soviet system had been anticipated by numerous writers, the disintegration of the USSR as a geopolitical entity was determined by a separate set of factors which, though in the final days ultimately related, had a logic of their own.

The search for the origins of 'totalitarianism' continues. Although a brilliant work in many respects, Hannah Arendt's take on the issue in her *The Origins of Totalitarianism* [4] has little of substance to say about the development of communism in Russia, especially since she stressed the role of pan-Slavism as the counterpart of pan-Germanism. Pan-Slavism, however, is very different and played almost no role in fostering great Russian nationalism, which (like anti-Semitism) is not a major tributary of Soviet authoritarianism. She was careful not to implicate Marx in the development of the despotic features of the communist order, although she did make some highly pertinent points about the necessitarian aspects of his thinking and the absence of a developed concept of individual political freedom, which tended to be submerged in collective processes.

Equally, the argument made by Jacob Talmon in his *The Origins of Totalitarian Democracy* [174] that Soviet ideology drew its provenance from the Enlightenment draws a misleading picture of developments in eighteenth-century European philosophy. Even on the continent the Enlightenment was far from monolithic, and the messianic strain was not predominant, and neither was the belief in the ability of conscious political intervention to shape the future and individuals [116]. The line from Rousseau to Lenin is a tenuous one. The line from Plato to Stalin is even less clear, although Karl Popper in his brilliant but perverse two-volume work on *The Open Society and its Enemies* [132] sought to demonstrate an intellectual filiation. Once the Soviet system had dissolved, however, no end of Russian commentary sought to portray communism in Russia as totalitarian, although by then the term was used with little nuance. As Gleason observes, if the origins of Soviet totalitarianism were imported through the bacillus of foreign ideologies, then Russia's responsibility was mitigated; but if the origins lay in Russia itself, then the problem could be cured by rejoining the west [59: *216*].

The reason for the intensely coercive nature of communism in Russia remains to be explained. In part it was derived from the nature of revolutionary politics. In the early 1790s the French revolution had taken a sharply terroristic form as the Committee of Public Safety under Robespierre sentenced thousands to the guillotine, all the while proclaiming that this served the liberation of humanity from oppression. The Jacobin terror served as a model for Lenin, although Soviet coercion was couched in the language of class. The Bolsheviks also had the example of the fate of the Paris Commune of 1871 before them, when following the defeat of the communards thousands were slaughtered by the forces of 'law and order'. Terror was far from the preserve of the totalitarian regimes of left and right. However, while certainly not unique to communist regimes, all such systems to a greater or lesser extent have relied on mass coercion to remain in power and achieve their goals. The imposition of communist regimes in eastern Europe after 1945 extended the Leninist–Stalinist system of systemic coercion, although after 1956 in a number of countries this was tempered. In China the huge losses provoked by the Great Leap Forward from 1958 were compounded by the extraordinary outbreak of 'popular terror' in the form of the Cultural Revolution from 1966. Cuba was at the moderate end of the spectrum in terms of mass coercion, but even here heavy-handed control mechanisms were prevalent. The justification was that a hostile United States was next door, and, indeed, the failure of the communist revolution to become a genuinely global phenomenon meant that it had to coexist with states that would welcome the demise of the non-capitalist systems. Vigilance in the face of capitalist revanchists was used to whip up the terror in Stalinist Russia, yet one suspects that even if, in some parallel universe, the capitalist states had disappeared the terror would have been little less virulent.

The communist experiment in Russia was tragic in the profound sense of the term: an idea that was to provide for the total liberation of humanity from exploitation and contingency led to the total enslavement of a population. The outcome was already implicit in the aim, although this is not to suggest that Stalinism was the only possible outcome. To see Lenin and Stalin as no more than vindictive criminals who were able by cunning and ruthlessness alone to seize and hold on to power is to miss the tragic element of the Soviet experience. It is not only a question of unintended consequences, but of knowing the consequences (and indeed embracing them) while remaining loyal to the belief in the emancipatory potential of the ideal – a theme Koestler explored in his *Darkness at Noon* (1940). This tension affected not only the early Bolshevik leaders but generations of communist sympathisers in the west as well, who were less constrained by immediate political needs yet still were trapped by the logic of trying to reconcile moral and political categories [26]. Soviet socialism was based on the ideal of a social revolution that potentially gave it a base of support beyond Russia itself, since that ideal had in the first place been generated in the west.

The totalitarian model suggests that, in very different ways, fascism, Nazism and communism were all variations of responses to the challenges of modernity, and in the post-communist era the differences between the right-wing and left-wing responses have been occluded, often for polemical purposes [29]. Sharing common roots in traditional social orders faced by the challenge of modernity, Soviet socialism proved more durable than its fascist counterpart. Both the tsarist and Soviet regimes were challenged by the twentieth century to adapt, and both were found wanting. In other European countries the responses were different: Italy turned to fascism, Spain was attracted by anarchism, and Germany finally took up Nazism. All in their own ways were responses to a comparable problem – late state-building in a competitive international environment, accompanied by intense conflicts over national identity and profound cultural challenges to what are perceived to be core civilisational characteristics. The Russian case was an extreme manifestation of this, and in certain respects the problem to which communism was one response has still not been resolved.

The rejection of allegedly utopian aspirations for human emancipation is the theme of James C. Scott's *Seeing Like a State* [155]. He casts such projects as Soviet collectivisation and compulsory Ujamaa villagisation in Tanzania as reflections of 'authoritarian high modernism', which combined 'the aspiration to the administrative ordering of nature and society' [155: *88*], 'the unrestrained use of the power of the modern state as an instrument for achieving these designs' [155: *88–9*] and the weakened capacity of civil society to resist these plans. High modernism for him is a strong version of linear beliefs in progress and modernisation that characterised western Europe and America up to the First World War. It is 'a particularly sweeping vision of how the benefits of technical and scientific progress might be applied – usually through the state – in every field of human activity' [155: *90*]. The historical basis of the argument is a powerful one; but the corollary that purposive state action is necessarily destructive is one that reflects the anti-statist dynamic of the ideology of globalisation, itself an ideology that was born of the fall of communism in Russia.

The gradualist thesis, or the evolutionary approach to social change, has now triumphed. While clearly this has developed in reaction to the terrors of the radical changes associated with the Jacobin/Bolshevik tradition, the repudiation of a whole historical epoch reaching back to the Enlightenment has enormous theoretical and political consequences. The idea of revolution, as Koselleck noted, imbued time with purpose and direction, and thus inspired generations with a sense that the flow of time was intelligible and that human intervention was purposeful and effective. A revolution marked the passage from one condition to another, which for the revolutionaries marked the transcendence of former inadequacies and through civil war entailed a rupture in historical development. The revolution in which the 'subjects themselves become the rulers', as Arendt put it (quoted in [94: *44*]), has now given way to a period in which the idea of 'anti-revolution' permeates social consciousness [152]. The anti-revolution repudiates the revolutionary method of achieving social change and historical justice, but it is not necessarily reactionary. It opposes the logic of revolution and not just the determinate features of a specific revolution, and is therefore more than simply a counter-revolution [36: *105*]. Its basic spirit has been well described by Gorbachev and Ikeda in their book of discussions [62], which at root urged a spiritual assessment of the communist experience. Although they stressed the positive spiritual charge of the new epoch, the burden of expectation has noticeably declined and it is difficult to retrieve a sense of 'genuine human history' [92: *45*].

By the end of the twentieth century the notion of emancipatory revolutionism had lost whatever popular resonance it once might have had in the countries that claimed to be building communism. Thus the events of 1989–91, when one eastern European country after another shook off the communist power systems, represented not only the overthrow of a specific regime type but also the repudiation of the social philosophy of emancipatory revolution on which they were based. It was this, as much as the geopolitical rearrangement of the international order that they entailed, that rendered these events epochal. At the same time, the fall of the Russian political project based on Marxian notions of emancipatory revolutionism discredited earlier ideas about Enlightenment revolutionism, and indeed Enlightenment ideas as a whole. Although the anti-communist revolutions took place under the banner of the assertion of neo-Kantian themes about the priority of human values above those of universal projects, Kant's thinking was itself a paean to rational humanism that has attracted fierce criticism for its sterile understanding of the delicate tissues of faith, belief and social solidarity that make up a coherent political community.

The CPSU proved to contain its own antithesis, the notion of reform communism, but this antithesis turned out to be not only to the Soviet communist party but to the whole trajectory of the communist movement from its inception in the mid-nineteenth century. Reform communism proved not to be a viable political option, something which Max Weber called 'an acceptable alternative', a different vision of how the political community could be organised. Instead, the only alternative on offer to Russia in 1991 was the modernity prevalent in the west, which became the programme of the anti-communist revolutionaries by default. The end of the communist revolution opened the way for a no less revolutionary transformation of society, driven forward by westernist liberals who sought to root the political changes of 1985–93 in a new socioeconomic order. The developmental achievements of the communist order were belittled, and at the same time it was replaced by a no less revolutionary system. It was capitalism that was ceaselessly radical, changing lives and social relations with an implacable logic.

The triumph of the anti-revolution does not, of course, mean the end of social and political tensions. Indeed, the end of the political and ideological paralysis induced by the Cold War (in both its domestic and international forms) restores the question of democratic renewal and the reach of politics to the centre of debate in the developed democracies. Freed from the incubus of revolutionary dreams of communist emancipation, offering apparently radical solutions that turn out to be no solutions at all, ruling elites can at last be challenged by genuinely radical questions of power and legitimacy. The sources of such a critique, however, remain unclear, and, as Leo Panitch and Sam Gindin note [124], the socialist failures of the past century have induced timidity in envisioning a future in which the homogenising and destructive power of global capitalism is challenged.

Russia and communism: an internal clash of civilisations

'The ship sank while entering port': these were the words of Winston Churchill on Russia in 1917. In his view Russia would have become the number one power in the capitalist world, but the Bolsheviks capsized the ship of state. Stolypin's reform programme was predicated on the emergence of a new class of peasant landowners who would provide the social support for a modernised regime. This class, however, was only embryonic in 1906, and was developing only slowly in the years to 1917. In other words, authoritarian modernisation required the support of a class that could only emerge as a result of that modernisation. The logical impossibility of being both cause and effect of a social revolution was to be a pattern repeated at least two more times in twentieth-century Russia. Equally, Russian history is often interpreted as one stage preparing for the next; with the tsarist regime laying down a cultural foundation on which the Soviet Union built, and the communist period establishing a set of political practices that have continued into the post-communist era. There is some sense in looking at history in this way, but such an approach tends to occlude disjuncture and innovation while exaggerating Russia's uniqueness. While a starkly binary approach may be a trait of Russian political culture, it is certainly not absent elsewhere. Bolshevism did more than exaggerate intrinsic authoritarian traits of Russian political culture; it elevated them to a whole new level. The double dissolution at the end of the twentieth century – of communism and the state in which it was contained – entailed a double reconstitution in which Russia remains engaged.

Seldom in history has a nation imposed such catastrophic losses upon itself. As perestroika unfolded, the sheer scale of the destruction unleashed by its rulers upon Russia was revealed. The Civil War ended with famine on the Volga, collectivisation was also accompanied by famine and the mass resettlement of peasants, the great terror swallowed the lives of a generation, while victory in the Second World War was achieved at an enormous and wasteful cost of lives. There was also the damage done to morality. As one of the early Bolshevik leaders, Georgi Piatakov, put it, 'If the Party demands it... I will see black where I thought I saw white... because for me there is no life outside the Party' (quoted in [71: *219*]). The Hungarian philosopher Georgy Lukacs made no bones about the intellectual sacrifice involved: 'The highest duty for communist ethics is to accept the necessity of acting immorally. This is the greatest sacrifice that the revolution demands of us. The conviction of the true communist is that evil transforms itself into bliss through the dialectics of historical evolution' (quoted in [71: *221*]). It was for this reason that in his *Letter to the Soviet Leaders* (5 September 1973) Alexander Solzhenitsyn called on them to 'cast off this cracked ideology':

> This universal, obligatory force-feeding with lies is now the most agonizing aspect of existence in our country – worse than all our material miseries, worse than any lack of civil liberties.
>
> All these arsenals of lies, which are totally unnecessary for our stability *as a state* [italics in original], are levied as a kind of tax for the benefit of ideology – to nail down events as they happen and clamp them to a tenacious, sharp-clawed but dead ideology: and it is precisely because our state, through sheer force of habit, tradition and inertia, continues to cling to this false doctrine with all its tortuous aberrations, that it needs to put the dissenter behind bars, for a false *ideology* can find no other answer to argument and protest than weapons and prison bars. [162: *47*]

It was this ideology, far more than economic policies or political organisation, that in Solzhenitsyn's view characterised the Soviet system since 1917, and he considered that it would be in their own best interests to drop the ideological baggage that was weighing them down [187: *483*]. His argument, which with hindsight appears almost preternaturally simple and right, is that by casting off the incubus of ideology the state could be saved. By the time Gorbachev engaged in such an exercise (although perestroika remained permeated with the ideology of reform communism), it was too late and both the system dissolved *and* the state disintegrated.

As far as Solzhenitsyn was concerned, it was the February revolution in 1917 that opened the door for subsequent catastrophes. On the ninetieth anniversary of the downfall of the autocracy in 2007 he published an article on the subject, written in 1980–3 but not published in his massive opus on the Russian revolution, *The Red Wheel* [166]. He condemned revolution as a form of change, and noted that even avowed monarchists betrayed the tsar in those sad days, and thus the revolution was successful not because of its overwhelming power but because of the weakness of the defenders of the monarchy. As Solzhenitsyn writes, 'Who could have predicted that the most powerful empire in the world would collapse with such speed; that a three hundred-year dynasty and a five hundred-year monarchy would fall without the slightest attempt to defend itself?' His trenchant critique of liberals and almost everyone else for overthrowing the monarchy provoked a discussion that raised important issues of relevance for our study of communism in Russia. The typical criticism was that Solzhenitsyn was too mild in his portrayal of Nicholas II, who had allowed the crisis to develop since at least 1915. The key point of Solzhenitsyn's argument is that Russian communism was born out of the inadequacies of the Provisional Government and was in no way an organic outcome of the course of Russian history. He drew the parallels with perestroika, noting that 'the political naivety, inexperience and irresponsibility before the country of Gorbachev's administration is striking. This was not power, but its senseless capitulation' [167: 5].

Yakovlev at the first conference of the Democratic Russia movement in late September 1991 argued: 'We have to catch up with civilisation, after missing out two entire eras – the post-industrial age and the information age. The result of that has been to put a curse on our society and its living standards, to dull people's souls, ostracise intellect and open the door to mob rule.' He went on:

> Trotsky once described Russia as 'an abominable thing which, like an armful of dry branches, should be thrown into the fire of the world revolution'. And in that cause, the lumpen-revolutionaries created a lumpen-socialism: state feudalism, with collective-farm serfdom, forced labour and permanent reprisals against intellectuals. The power monopoly seized a monopoly on property, under rabidly anti-bourgeois slogans – not realising that a new society could only be post-bourgeois, not anti-bourgeois.

He argued the Marxist utopias shaped the country after the revolution, above all in the destruction of the institutions of civil society and in the repudiation of traditional ways of managing the labour process. In the end, he insisted, 'Bolshevik communism ... lost its dispute with history', and it did so 'because of these and many other original sins, which it carried in its genes from the very start'. He argued that the Soviet system before perestroika resembled a 'slave-owning society, in terms of how mutual interests and the entire system of economic and social motivation were built into it' [193: 6].

Did the Bolshevik revolution in Russia achieve at least a modicum of modernisation and the fulfilment of strategic goals that could not have been achieved at less cost by other means? In other words, was communism in Russia necessary? A similar question is asked about the French revolution [147]; and Alec Nove raised the same issue when he asked 'Was Stalin Really Necessary?' [118]. The Bolshevik revolution represented the exemplary case of a giant boot-strapping operation, an authoritarian modernisation based on the politics of levitation. Marxist revolutions, with certain qualifications, assumed that socialism would come after capitalism, yet Lenin's theory of imperialism sought to finesse the problem of Russia's relative backwardness by arguing that the revolution would spread to the more advanced countries which would then come to Russia's aid. The Russian working class, the theoretical subject of the revolution, was marginalised both politically and theoretically. Placed in a condition of political dependency after the revolution, when the class did indeed become the dominant social group in society as a result of Stalinist industrialisation, it was never allowed to develop as an autonomous political force. Although the working class was formally the privileged class in the Soviet Union, and this was reflected in some tangible political and social benefits, the declaration in the post-Stalin era that the system had become an 'all-people's state' meant that its status was diluted.

At the heart of the Russian revolution was the attempt to find new ways of resolving developmental challenges. As in other modernising states, notably Japan and China, there was a profound tension between economic modernisation (which ultimately entails westernisation) and the preservation of sociocultural and civilisational identity. The Leninist inflexion of modernity was an original attempt to resolve this issue, and it is on this basis that contemporary Russian patriots defend the communist experience. Although internationalist in ideology, from the very first the Bolshevik revolution was primarily about Russia. In other words, the whole project of communism in Russia was torn by an internal clash of civilisations: between the communist (Leninist) civilisation that was struggling to be born, based on non-capitalist principles while seeking to fulfil the promise of the Enlightenment, and Russian civilisation, which sought to preserve its distinct identity and traditions. Soviet Russia became, to use Huntington's term, a spectacular example of a 'cleft country' [74: *209*]. In the early period the clash was gargantuan, with the destruction of fundamental aspects of Russia's civilisation, notably the Russian Orthodox Church and other traditional religions, together with peasant culture. During the war and with increasing intensity thereafter the two civilisations began to merge, interspersed with moments of the militant recrudescence of the communist civilisation, notably during Khrushchev's revivalist anti-religious crusade from 1959. However, a fully-fledged synthesis in the form of a new 'Soviet civilisation' was not created, and instead the power system became increasingly isolated from the society and the nations that it sought to rule.

However, it would not be possible, despite the dramatic negative mobilisation in 1989–91, for Russia to slough off communism as a snake sheds its skin. Communist rule may have ended in 1991, but the long shadow of seven decades of socialist experimentation could not be discarded so easily. Indeed, it was unclear where communism ended and Russia began. A study by the Levada analytical agency found that as late as 2005 26 per cent of respondents considered that the October revolution had 'opened up a new era in the history of the peoples of Russia' (up from 23 per cent in 1990), while 31 per cent considered that it had promoted social and economic development (26 per cent in 1990), while the contrary view that it had impeded their development was shared by 16 per cent (18 per cent in 1990), and only 15 per cent (12 per cent in 1990) considered that it had been catastrophic. There was a marked age profile to the responses, with those over forty more inclined to take a positive view. Astonishingly, when asked what they would do if the October revolution took place today, 17 per cent would give active support, 17 per cent would cooperate, 28 per cent would stand on the sidelines and hope to survive, while only 7 per cent would actively oppose the revolution, and another 14 per cent would flee abroad [103]. The revolution had sunk deep roots in Russia, and, while the older generation retained greater sympathy, the level of support across the board is surprising. Lenin, indeed, is seen by many as a leading statist and the saviour of Russia, 'transferring the capital [in March 1918] from dead Petersburg to magnificent Moscow. He returned Russia home' [121: *15*].

Lenin commented that Peter the Great had tried to modernise Russia by barbaric means, and this applies equally to the Bolsheviks. The paradox of the Petrine reforms in the early eighteenth century has often been remarked upon: in trying to accelerate Russia's modernisation on the Western pattern, Peter in fact retarded the organic development of society and the polity. He is charged with opening up an unbridgeable gulf between the bureaucracy and the ruled ('dual Russia'), and thus set in motion a series of contradictions that were, if not resolved, at least superseded by the October revolution of 1917. This paradox, whereby the attempt to impose accelerated change from above only accentuates the archaic political features of the regime, borrowing western technology and models but losing in translation the very spirit of these techniques and institutions that gave them life, is one that was repeated at least twice in the twentieth century. Communist development represented modernisation without the spirit of modernity, that is, the open-ended search for something approximating the truth, the spirit of critical enquiry and independence, and the dynamism that is associated with a thriving market. Yeltsin's reforms once again borrowed the whole panoply of institutional devices from the west, in the sphere of politics, society and the economy, yet something artificial remained in their adaptation to Russian conditions, reflected in the various traumas in two decades of the great democratic experiment.

The eighteenth-century reforms, for all their contradictions, set in motion a developmental process that lasted for two centuries, whereas the Leninist challenge was remarkably short-lived. Gorbachev's reform communism, as implemented during perestroika, demonstrated that there was no sustainable Leninist basis for the renewal of the system, and thus the twin and interlinked processes of dissolution and disintegration gathered force and culminated in the destruction of both the system and the state in 1991. In the longer term, Soviet-style mis-modernisation could have continued indefinitely, but more effective modernisation, as the Chinese discovered, would have entailed the injection of increasing doses of the market which would have ultimately eroded the non-capitalist bases of the system. Equally, the Soviet stability system could have inserted more elements from the armoury of ordered societies: above all some sort of match between goals and resources; the convergence of the reality propounded at the official level and the lived reality of the mass of the people; functioning feedback mechanisms from society that could in a non-populist manner shape policy; and the creation of more effective mechanisms to achieve adaptive innovation.

The clash between two versions of progressive modernity at the interstate level took the form of the Cold War, itself a form of the clash of civilisations that Huntington mistakenly asserted was a post-Cold War phenomenon; but there was no less a domestic cold war that took the form of a civil war between two civilisations. We have argued earlier that the thesis of the Russification of Marxism has to be modified by awareness that many of the features of communism in Russia did in fact draw on aspects of Marxism, and thus any simplistic notion that Russia took a fully-formed emancipatory system and proceeded to implement a vulgarised form has to be discounted. However, the Lenin–Stalin version certainly exploited the contradictions in Marxism to create a particularly terroristic and alienating form of communism. Leninist communism, certainly, was made possible and reinforced by Russian conditions, but the philosophy and practices of the new state represented a stark repudiation of the fundamental values of the old system. Lenin–Stalin civilisation came into contradiction with Russian civilisation, but the two cannot be hermetically separated and by the end became mutually reinforcing. This is one of the legacies of the communist era that has not yet been resolved in post-communist Russia.

Russia after communism

Russia left the twentieth century in much the same way as it entered: lagging behind the more advanced societies economically, unsure of its way forward, facing enormous social crises and unable to find a satisfactory way of bringing together its various nations to make a single political community, with its politics secretive and arbitrary, occasionally vicious and xenophobic, and its place amongst the community of nations endlessly questioned by itself and others. The enormous sacrifices in war and revolution appeared to have achieved little benefit to the country, and what had been achieved was done at great cost.

While other countries suffered as much as Russia in the collective fantasies of the first part of the century, with Japan and Germany having engaged in militaristic advantages that by 1945 left them in ruins, in the second half of the century those two countries and the rest of western Europe were transformed from essentially rural peasant societies into modern comfortable economies governed within the framework of liberal democracy. China, having endured humiliation at the hands of foreigners following the Boxer rebellion of 1899–1902 and three-quarters of a century of civil conflict, from the last decades of the twentieth century enjoyed unprecedented economic growth and relative political stability. Russia, of all the great powers, alone appears not to have found a formula that could translate its potential into reality. Why is this so? What is it about Russia that makes it perpetually modernising but never modernised, always catching up but never overtaking?

Moderate and right-wing Russian nationalists alike see the source of communism in the morbidities of western bourgeois capitalism. The Stalinist phenomenon was not an exclusively Russian problem and 'cannot be fully understood unless it is treated as part of Western intellectual history' [95: *172*]. Communism came to eastern Europe from the Soviet Union; hence the 'return to Europe' of these countries is relatively straightforward since their rejection of communism is reinforced by their rejection of Soviet/Russian imperialism [60]. In Russia, however, communism came from the west, and the rejection of the former in many cases only serves to reinforce the traditional rejection of the latter. Already in 1918 Izgoyev in *Iz glubiny* had rejected the argument that socialism in Russia had failed because of the mistakes and excesses of the Bolsheviks themselves, and insisted that socialism itself was to blame. By the early 1920s Lenin and Trotsky tried to shift the burden of failure on to the Russian people, as somehow Asiatic, bureaucratic, barbaric and altogether unworthy of the great gift that the Bolsheviks proffered them through the slaughter of countless millions and the destruction of independent intellectuals and institutions.

While Slavophiles might suggest a mystical answer, that Russia's sufferings were intended to show the world the way of sacrifice and humility and how not to do things, this is an answer (while true in its own way) that hardly satisfies the more inquisitive and rationalistic mind. Harder-edged Russian nationalists would seek the answer in the world of conspiracy, in the west's refusal to accept Russia for what it is, fearing indeed Russia's unique mission in the world (quite what that mission is, other than to be treated as an equal, is never made entirely clear), and thus the great powers of the west (now including Japan) have spent the last century (and longer) opposing Russia at every turn, and then seized the opportunity offered by Gorbachev's capitulation during perestroika and by the romantic democrats after 1991 to drive home the advantage to reduce Russia to no more than a 'raw materials appendage' of the west. Once again, there is an element of truth in this account, written up most effectively by Solzhenitsyn in his *The Russian Question at the End of the Twentieth Century* [164].

The argument, moreover, that western pressure forced the Soviet Union to launch its reforms, and that in some way western powers 'won' the Cold War, reflects a totally inappropriate triumphalism. Soviet reforms were launched as a response to domestic developments and normative concerns, and outside powers were at best marginal in the process [18; 19]. The west missed the opportunity to build a lasting relationship of trust at the end of the Cold War in 1988–92, failing to offer sufficient intelligent economic and moral assistance and support, and instead in 1994 began the process of NATO enlargement and other actions that once again isolated Russia [154]. Yet it would be quite wrong to lay the main responsibility for Russian failures anywhere else other than in Russia itself. To do so would be to heap yet more humiliation on to Russia, as a country unable even to take responsibility for its own destiny other than in murderous intervals of aggressive imperialism, unable to find a peaceful and equitable way of interacting with its neighbours and the world.

The repudiation of communism in Russia represents a revolt against utopia, but this does not necessarily mean the death of aspirations of a more just order – only the revolutionary version of such an order. The death of the revolutionary concept of consciousness does not entail the death of autonomy but precisely its vindication through a new appreciation of the role of spirituality in society. Without necessarily accepting his thesis on 'the boredom at the end of history', Fukuyama describes a type of postmodern politics in which Marxist class politics is replaced by Nietzschean concerns for authenticity and autonomy (*thymos*) [50]. The anti-revolutions put an end to the trajectory of westernising and modernising revolutions, but the revolutionary problematic has not disappeared. This can be defined as the tension between an existing order, which by definition claims to represent civilisation, and an alternative order *in statu nascendi*, which denounces the artificiality of the present in the name of a more profound rationality that can be achieved by the revolutionary restoration of nature, the underlying natural order corresponding to human nature and society. While the Bolshevik version of communism in Russia had limited potential for positive transcendence, the agenda of the Russian revolution is by no means over.

References

[1]   Adams, Bruce, *Tiny Revolutions in Russia: Twentieth-Century Soviet and Russian History in Anecdotes* (London and New York, RoutledgeCurzon, 2005).

[2]   Amalrik, Andrei, *Will the Soviet Union Survive until 1984?* (Harmondsworth, Penguin, 1970).

[3]   Applebaum, Anne, *Gulag: A History of the Soviet Concentration Camps* (London, Penguin, 2003).

[4]   Arendt, Hannah, *The Origins of Totalitarianism* (New York, Harcourt, 1994 [1951]).

[5]   Arnason, Johann P., *The Future that Failed: Origins and Destinies of the Soviet Model* (London, Routledge, 1993).

[6]   Aron, Raymond, *18 Lectures on Industrial Society* (London, Widenfeld & Nicolson, 1967).

[7]   Avrich, Paul, *Kronstadt 1921* (Princeton, NJ, Princeton University Press, 1970).

[8]   Bakunin, Michael, *Statism and Anarchy*, translated and edited by Marshall S. Shatz (Cambridge, Cambridge University Press, 1990).

[9]   Barros, James, and Richard Gregor, *Double Deception: Stalin, Hitler, and the Invasion of Russia* (DeKalb, ILL, Northern Illinois University Press, 2009).

[10] Bauman, Zygmunt, *Modernity and the Holocaust* (Ithaca, Cornell University Press, 1989).

[11] Beissinger, Mark, 'The Persisting Ambiguity of Empire', *Post-Soviet Affairs*, Vol. 11, No. 2, 1995, pp. 149–84.

[12] Berdyaev, Nikolai, *The Meaning of History*, Introduction by Maria Nemcova Banerjee (New Brunswick, Transaction Publishers, 2005 [1934]).

[13] Berliner, Joseph, *Soviet Industry from Stalin to Gorbachev: Essays on Management and Innovation* (Aldershot, Edward Elgar, 1988).

[14] Besançon, Alain, *Glasnost'*, No. 13 (1988), p. 19.

[15] Bisley, Nick, *The End of the Cold War and the Causes of Soviet Collapse* (Basingstoke, Palgrave Macmillan, 2004).

[16] Boobbyer, Philip, *Conscience, Dissent and Reform in Soviet Russia* (London, Routledge, 2005).

[17] Bracke, Maud, *Which Socialism, Whose Détente? West European Communism and the Czechoslovak Crisis of 1968* (Budapest, Central European University Press, 2007).

[18] Brown, Archie, *The Gorbachev Factor* (Oxford, Oxford University Press, 1996).

[19] Brown, Archie, 'Perestroika and the End of the Cold War', *Cold War History*, Vol. 7, No. 1, February 2007, pp. 1–17.

[20] Brown, Archie, *The Rise and Fall of Communism* (London, Bodley Head, 2009).

[21] Brudny, Yitzhak M., *Reinventing Russia: Russian Nationalism and the Soviet State, 1953–1991* (Cambridge, MA, Harvard University Press, 1999).

[22] Bukharin, N. and E. Preobrazhensky, *ABC of Communism*, introduction by E. H. Carr (Harmondsworth, Penguin Books, 1969).

[23] Bulgakov, Sergei, ' Heroism and Ascetism', in Marshall S. Shatz and Judith E. Zimmerman (eds), *Vekhi: Landmarks – a Collection of Articles about the Russian Intelligentsia* (Armonk, M. E. Sharpe, 1994), pp. 17–49.

[24] Bunce, Valerie, *Subversive Institutions: The Design and the Destruction of Socialism and the State* (Cambridge, Cambridge University Press, 1999).

[25] Butt, V. P., A. B. Murphy, N. A. Myshovand G. R. Swain (eds), *The Russian Civil War: Documents from the Soviet Archives* (New York, St Martin's Press, 1996).

[26] Caute, David, *The Fellow-Travellers: Intellectual Friends of Communism* (New Haven, CT, Yale University Press, 1988).

[27] Chalidze, Valery, *To Defend These Rights: Human Rights and the Soviet Union* (New York, Random House, 1974).

[28] Conquest, Robert, 'Victims of Stalinism: A Comment', *Europe-Asia Studies*, Vol. 49, No. 7, 1997, pp. 1317–1319.

[29] Courtois, Stéphane, Nicola Werth, Jean-Louis Panné, Andrzej Paczkowski, Karel Bartosek and Jean-Louis Margolin, *The Black Book of Communism: Crimes, Terror, Repression* (Cambridge, MA, Harvard University Press, 1999).

[30] Cox, Michael (ed.), *Rethinking Soviet Collapse: Sovietology, the Death of Communism and the New Russia* (London and New York, Pinter, 1998).

[31] Custine, Marquis De, *Letters From Russia* (London, Penguin Books, 1991).

[32] Daly, Jonathan W., *The Watchful State: Security Police and Opposition in Russia, 1906–1917* (DeKalb, Northern Illinois University Press, 2004).

[33] Daniels, Robert V., *The End of the Communist Revolution* (London, Routledge, 1993).

[34] Danilevskii, N. Ya., *Rossiya i Evropa* (Moscow, Kniga, 1991 [1871]).

[35] Davies, Joseph E., *Mission to Moscow* (London, Victor Gollancz, 1942).

[36] de Maistre, Joseph, 'Supposed Dangers of Counter-Revolution', in Joseph de Maistre, *Considerations on France* (Cambridge, Cambridge University Press, 1994), pp. 83–105.

[37] *Diderot et Catherine II* (Paris, J. M. Tourneux, 1899).

[38] Djilas, Milovan, *The New Class: An Analysis of the Communist System* (New York, Praeger, 1957).

[39] Duncan, Peter, *Russian Messianism: Third Rome, Revolution, Communism and After* (London, Routledge, 2000).

[40] Dunham, Vera, *In Stalin's Time* (Cambridge, MA, Harvard University Press, 1979).

[41] Dunlop, John B., *The Rise of Russia and the Fall of the Soviet Empire* (Princeton, NJ, Princeton University Press, 1993).

[42] Dunn, John, 'Revolution?', in his *Western Political Theory in the Face of the Future* (Cambridge, Cambridge University Press, 1979).

[43] Eisenstadt, S. N., *Modernisation: Protest and Change* (Englewood Cliffs, NJ, Prentice-Hall, 1966).

[44] Eley, Geoff, 'History With the Politics Left Out- Again?', *The Russian Review*, Vol. 45, 1986, pp. 385–394.

[45] Farber, Samuel, *Before Stalinism: The Rise and Fall of Soviet Democracy* (London, Verso, 1990).

[46] Fehér, Ferenc, Agnes Heller and György Márkus, *Dictatorship over Needs: An Analysis of Soviet Societies* (Oxford, Blackwell, 1983).

[47] Fitzpatrick, Sheila, 'New Perspectives on Stalinism', *The Russian Review*, Vol. 45, 1986, pp. 357–373.

[48] Fitzpatrick, Sheila, *The Cultural Front* (Ithaca, Cornell University Press, 1992).

[49] Friedman, Edward, 'Modernization and Democratization in Leninist States: The Case of China', *Studies in Comparative Communism*, Vol. 22, No. 2/3, Summer/Autumn 1989, pp. 251–64.

[50] Fukuyama, Francis, *The End of History and the Last Man* (London, Penguin Books, 1992).

[51] Furet, François, *The Passing of an Illusion : the Idea of Communism in the Twentieth Century* (Chicago, University of Chicago Press, 2000).

[52] Furman, Dmitrii, 'Revolyutsionnye tsikly Rossii', *Svobodnaya mysl'*, No. 1, 1994.

[53] Gane, Mike (ed.), *The Radical Sociology of Durkheim and Mauss* (London, Routledge, 1992).

[54] Gatrell, Peter, *Government, Industry and Rearmament in Russia, 1900–1914: The Last Argument of Tsarism* (Cambridge, Cambridge University Press, 1994).

[55] Gerschenkron, A., *Economic Backwardness in Historical Perspective* (Cambridge, MA, Harvard University Press, 1962).

[56] Getty, J. Arch, *Origins of the Great Purges: The Soviet Communist Party Reconsidered, 1933–1938* (Cambridge, Cambridge University Press, 1985).

[57] Getty, J. Arch and Oleg V. Naumov, *Yezhov: The Rise of Stalin's 'Iron Fist'* (New Haven, CT, Yale University Press, 2008).

[58] Gilligan, Emma, *Defending Human Rights in Russia: Sergei Kovalyov, Dissident and Human Rights Commissioner, 1969–2003* (London, RoutledgeCurzon, 2004).

[59] Gleason, Abbott, *Totalitarianism: The Inner History of the Cold War* (New York and Oxford, Oxford University Press, 1995).

[60] Glenny, Misha, *The Rebirth of History: Eastern Europe in the Age of Democracy* (London, Penguin Books, 1990).

[61] Gorbachev, Mikhail, *Perestroika: New Thinking for our Country and the World* (London, Collins, 1987).

[62] Gorbachev, Mikhail and Daisaku Ikeda, *Moral Lessons of the Twentieth Century: Gorbachev and Ikeda on Buddhism and Communism* (London, I. B. Tauris, 2005).

[63] Gramsci, Antonio, *Selections from the Prison Notebooks* (London, Lawrence & Wishart, 1971).

[64] Gray, John, *Enlightenment's Wake: Politics and Culture at the Close of the Modern Age* (London and New York, Routledge, 1995).

[65] *Guardian*, 14 December1991.

[66] Habermas, Jürgen, 'What Does Socialism Mean Today? The Rectifying Revolution and the Need for New Thinking on the Left', *New Left Review*, No. 183 (September/October 1990), pp. 3–21.

[67] Habermas, Jürgen, *The Structural Transformation of the Public Sphere: An Inquiry into a Category of Bourgeois Society*, Introduced by Thomas McCarthy (Cambridge, Polity Press, 2006 [1962]).

[68] Halfin, Igal, *Intimate Enemies: Demonizing the Bolshevik Opposition, 1918–1928* (Pittsburgh, University of Pittsburgh Press, 2007).

[69] Hayek, F. A., *The Fatal Conceit: The Errors of Socialism* (London, Routledge, 1988).

[70] Hoffman, John, 'The Coercion/Consent Analysis of the State under Socialism', in Neil Harding (ed.), *The State in Socialist Society* (London, Macmillan, 1984), pp. 129–49.

[71] Hollander, Paul, *Political Will and Personal Belief: The Decline and fall of Soviet Communism* New Haven and London, Yale University Press, 1999).

[72] Hosking, Geoffrey, *Russia: People and Empire 1552–1917* (London, Harper Collins, 1997).

[73] Hosking, Geoffrey, *Rulers and Victims: The Russian in the Soviet Union* (Cambridge, MA, Belknap, 2006).

[74] Huntington, Samuel P., *The Clash of Civilizations and the Remaking of World Order* (New York, Simon & Schuster, 1996).

[75] Inkeles, A., and D. H. Smith, *Becoming Modern: Individual Change in Six Developing Countries* (Cambridge, MA, Harvard University Press, 1974).

[76] *Iz glubiny: Sbornik statei o russkoi revolyutsii* (Moscow, Novosti, 1991).

[77] Jones, Adrian, *Late Imperial Russia: An Interpretation – Three Visions, Two Cultures, One Peasantry* (Bern, Peter Lang, 1997).

[78] Karpinski, Jakub, 'Roads from Communism', *Uncaptive Minds*, Summer 1994, Vol. 7, No. 2.

[79] Kassof, A., 'The Administered Society: Totalitarianism Without Terror', *World Politics*, Vol. 6, No. 4, July 1964, pp. 558–75.

[80] Kautsky, Karl, *The Dictatorship of the Proletariat* (Michigan, Ann Arbor Paperback, 1964).

[81] Keenan, Edward L., 'Muscovite Political Folkways', *The Russian Review*, Vol. 45, 1986, pp. 115–81.

[82]   Keep, John, '1917: Tyranny of Paris over Petrograd', *Soviet Studies*, Vol. 20, 1968–69.

[83]   Kennan, George (X), 'The Sources of Soviet Conduct', *Foreign Affairs*, July 1947, pp. 566–82.

[84]   Kharkhordin, Oleg, 'Chto Takoe "Gosudarstvo"?', in Oleg Kharkhordin, *Ponyatie gosudarstva v cheyrekh yazykakh* (St Petersburg & Moscow, European University of St Petersburg, 2002), pp. 152–217.

[85]   Khlevniuk, Oleg V., *Master of the House: Stalin and His Inner Circle* (New Haven, CT, Yale University Press, 2009).

[86]   Koestler, Arthur, *Arrow in the Blue: An Autobiography* (London, Collins, 1952).

[87]   Kolakowski, Leszek, 'The Myth of Human Self-Identity: Unity of Civil and Political Society in Socialist Thought', in Leszek Kolakowski and Stuart Hampshire (eds), *The Socialist Idea: A Reappraisal* (London, Weidenfeld & Nicolson, 1974), pp. 18–35.

[88]   Kollontai, Alexandra, *The Workers' Opposition in Russia* (London, Dreadnought Publishers, 1923).

[89]   Kolonitskii, Boris, ' "Democracy" in the Political Conscioussness of the February Revolution', *Slavic Review*, Vol. 57, No. 1, Spring 1998, pp. 95–106.

[90]   Kopelev, Lev, 'Stoletnyaya voina XX veka', *Moskovskie novosti*, No. 29, 23–30 April 1995, p. 5.

[91]   Kornai, János, *The Socialist System: The Political Economy of Communism* (Princeton, NJ, Princeton University Press, 1992).

[92]   Koselleck, Reinhart, *Futures Past: On the Semantics of Historical Time*, trans. by Keith Tribe, (Cambridge, MA, MIT Press, 1985 [1979]).

[93]   Koselleck, Reinhart, *Critique and Crisis: Enlightenment and the Pathogenesis of Modern Society* (Oxford, Berg, 1988).

[94]   Kotkin, Stephen, *Magnetic Mountain: Stalinism as a Civilisation* (California University Press, 1995).

[95]   Krasnov, Vladislav, *Russia Beyond Communism: A Chronicle of National Rebirth* (Boulder, Westview Press, 1991).

[96]   Kravchenko, Victor, *I Chose Freedom: The Personal and Political Life of a Soviet Official* (London, Robert Hale, 1947).

[97]   Kropotkin, P., 'Message to the Workers of the Western World', June 1920, in Marshall Shatz (ed.), *The Future of Bread and Other Writings* (Cambridge, Cambridge University Press, 1995).

[98]   Kumar, Krishan (ed.), *Revolution: The Theory and Practice of a European Idea* (London, Weidenfeld and Nicolson, 1971).

[99]   Kundera, Milan, 'The Tragedy of Central Europe', *New York Review of Books*, Vol. 31, No. 7, 26 April 1984, p. 33.

[100] Kuromiya, Hiroaki, *The Voices of the Dead: Stalin's Great Terror in the 1930s* (New Haven, Yale University Press, 2008).

[101] Ledeneva, Alena V., *Russia's Economy of Favours: Blat, Networking and Informal Exchange* (Cambridge, Cambridge University Press, 1998).

[102] Lefort, Claude, *Complications: Communism and the Dilemmas of Democracy* (New York, Columbia University Press, 2007).

[103] Levada-Centre, 'Otnoshenie rossiyan k Oktyabr'skoi revolyutsii 1917 goda', 3 November 2005, 1600 respondents for a poll conducted on 14–17 October 2005 in 46 regions, http://www.levada.ru/press/2005110301.html.

[104] Ligachev, Yegor, *Inside Gorbachev's Kremlin: The Memoirs of Yegor Ligachev* (Boulder, CO, Westview, 1996).

[105] Lih, Lars T., *Lenin Rediscovered? What is to Be Done? in Context* (Leiden, Brill, 2006).

[106] Lih, Lars T., Oleg V. Naumov and Oleg V. Khlevniuk (eds), *Stalin's Letters to Molotov, 1925–1936* (Fairhaven, CT, Yale University Press, 1995).

[107] Lovell, David W., *From Marx to Lenin: An Evaluation of Marx's Responsibility for Soviet Authoritarianism* (Cambridge, Cambridge University Press, 1984).

[108] Luxemburg, Rosa, *The Russian Revolution* (Ann Arbor, University of Michigan Press, 1961).

[109] Malia, Martin, (writing initially as 'Z'), 'To the Stalin Mausoleum', *Daedalus*, Vol. 169, No. 1 (Winter 1990), pp. 295–344; reprinted in Stephen R. Graubard (ed.), *Eastern Europe ... Central Europe ... Europe* (Boulder, Westview Press, 1991), pp. 283–338.

[110] Malia, Martin, *Russia under Western Eyes: From the Bronze Horseman to the Lenin Mausoleum* (Cambridge, Mass., Belknap, 2000).

[111] Martin, Terry, *The Affirmative Action Empire: Nations and Nationalism in the Soviet Union, 1923–1939* (Ithaca and London, Cornell University Press, 2001).

[112] Matejka, Zdenek, 'How the Warsaw Pact was Dissolved', *Perspectives: Institute of International Relations*, Prague, Summer 1997.

[113] Mauss, Marcel, 'A Sociological Assessment of Bolshevism (1924–5)', in Mike Gane (ed.), *The Radical Sociology of Durkheim and Mauss* (London, Routledge, 1992), pp. 165–211.

[114] Melancon, Michael, *The Lena Goldfields Massacre and the Crisis of the Late Tsarist State* (College Station, Texas A&M University Press, 2006).

[115] Murrell, Peter and Mancur Olson, *The Rise and Decline of Nations* (New Haven and London, Yale University Press, 1982).

[116] Neiman, Susan, *Moral Clarity: A Guide for Grown-Up Idealists* (London, Bodley Head, 2009).

[117] Nol'te, Ernst, *Evropeiskaya grazhdanskaya voina, 1917–1945: Natsional-sotsializm i Bol'shevizm* (*The European Civil War, 1917–1945: National Socialism and Bolshevism; Der Europaische Burgerkrieg 1917–1945: Nationalsozialismus und Bolschewismus*), Transl. from German by A. Antonovskii ed. and afterword by S. Zemlianoi (Moscow, Logos, 2003).

[118] Nove, Alec, *Economic Rationality and Soviet Politics, or Was Stalin Really Necessary?* (London, George Allen & Unwin, 1964).

[119] Nove, Alec, *An Economic History of the USSR* (Harmondsworth, Pelican, 1972).

[120] Nove, Alec, *The Economics of Feasible Socialism* (London, George Allen & Unwin, 1983).

[121] Ol'shanskii, Dmitrii, 'Kerzhenskii dukh, igumenskii okrik', *Konservator*, No. 14 (30), 18–24 April 2003, p. 15.

[122] Olson, Mancur, 'The Logic of Collective Action in Soviet-type Societies', *Journal of Soviet Nationalities*, No. 1, 1990.

[123] Overy, Richard, *The Morbid Age: Britain Between the Wars* (London, Allen Lane, 2009).

[124] Panitch, Leo and Sam Gindin, 'Transcending Pessimism: Rekindling Socialist Imagination', in Leo Panitch and Colin Leys (eds), *Necessary and Unnecessary Utopias: Socialist Register 2000* (Woodbridge, Merlin Press, 1999), pp. 1–29.

[125] Petro, Nicolai, *Crafting Democracy: How Novgorod has Coped with Rapid Social Change* (Ithaca, NY, Cornell University Press, 2004).

[126] Pipes, Richard (ed.), *The Russian Intelligentsia* (New York, Columbia University Press, 1961).

[127] Pipes, Richard, *The Russian Revolution* (New York, Random House, 1991).

[128] Pirani, Simon, *The Russian Revolution in Retreat, 1920–1924: Soviet Workers and the New Communist Elite* (London, Routledge, 2008).

[129] Pittey, Roderic, 'Imagining Liberation: Russian Critiques of Stalinism', *Debatte*, Vol. 17, No. 1, April 2009, pp. 99–116.

[130] Poe, Marshall T., *The Russian Moment in World History* (Princeton NJ, Princeton University Press, 2003).

[131] Polan, A. J., *Lenin and the End of Politics* (London, Methuen, 1984).

[132] Popper, K. R., *The Open Society and its Enemies*, Vol. 1, *The Spell of Plato*, Vol. 2, *The High Tide of Prophecy: Hegel, Marx, and the Aftermath* (London, Routledge & Kegan Paul, 1945).

[133] Porter, Roy, *The Enlightenment*, 2nd edn (Basingstoke, Palgrave Macmillan, 1990).

[134] Price, Morgan Philips, *Dispatches from the Revolution: Russia 1916–18*, edited by Tania Rose (London, Pluto Press, 1997).

[135] Priestland, David, *Stalinism and the Politics of Mobilization: Ideas, Power, and Terror in Inter-War Russia* (Oxford, Oxford University Press, 2007).

[136] Putin, Vladimir, *First Person: An Astonishingly Frank Self-Portrait by Russia's President Vladimir Putin*, with Nataliya Gevorkyan, Natalya Timakova, and Andrei Kolesnikov, translated by Catherine A. Fitzpatrick (London, Hutchinson, 2000).

[137] Raack, R. C., *Stalin's Drive to the West 1938–45: The Origins of the Cold War* (Cambridge, Cambridge University Press, 1995).

[138] Rakovski, Marc, *Towards an East European Marxism* (London, Alison & Busby, 1978).

[139] Rakowska-Harmstone, Teresa, 'The Dialectics of Nationalism in the USSR', *Problems of Communism*, Vol. 23, No. 3, May-June 1974, pp. 1–22.

[140] Ransome, Arthur, *Six Weeks in Russia, 1919* (London, Faber Finds, 2010).

[141] Reddaway, Peter and Dmitri Glinski, *The Tragedy of Russia's Reforms: Market Bolshevism against Democracy* (Washington, DC, The United States Institute of Peace Press, 2001).

[142] Remington, Thomas F., *Building Socialism in Bolshevik Russia: Ideology and Industrial Organization, 1917–1921* (University of Pittsburgh Press, 1984).

[143] Remnick, David, *Lenin's Tomb: The Last Days of the Soviet Empire* (London, Viking, 1993).

[144] Rittersporn, Gabor T. *Stalinist Simplifications and Soviet Complications: Social Tensions and Political Conflicts in the USSR, 1933–1953* (Philadelphia, Harwood Academic, 1991).

[145] Roeder, Philip G., *Red Sunset: The Failure of Soviet Politics* (Princeton, NJ, Princeton University Press, 1993).

[146] Rummel, R. J., *Lethal Politics: Soviet Genocide and Mass Murder since 1917* (New Brunswick, NJ, Transaction Publishers, 1996).

[147] Runciman, W. G., 'Unnecessary Revolution: The Case of France', *Archives Européennes de Sociologie*, Vol. 24, No. 2, 1983, pp. 291–318.

[148] Rupnik, Jacques, *The Other Europe* (London, Weidenfeld & Nicolson, 1989).

[149] Ruud, Charles, *Russian Entrepreneur: Publisher Ivan Sytin of Moscow, 1851–1934* (Montreal, McGill-Queen's University Press, 1990).

[150] Ryklin, Mikhail, *Svoboda i zapret: kul'tura v epokhu terrora* (Moscow, Logos, Progress-Traditsiya, 2008).

[151] Sakwa, Richard (ed.), *The Rise and Fall of the Soviet Union* (London, Routledge, 1999).

[152] Sakwa, Richard, 'The Age of Paradox: The Anti-revolutionary Revolutions of 1989–91', in Moira Donald and Tim Rees (eds), *Reinterpreting Revolution in Twentieth-Century Europe* (London, Macmillan, 2001), pp. 159–76.

[153] Sakwa, Richard, 'From Revolution To *Krizis*: The Transcending Revolutions of 1989–91', *Comparative Politics*, vol. 38, no. 4, 2006, pp. 459–78.

[154] Sakwa, Richard, ' "New Cold War" or Twenty Years' Crisis?: Russia and International Politics', *International Affairs*, Vol. 84, No. 2, March 2008, pp. 241–67.

[155] Scott, James C., *Seeing Like a State: How Certain Schemes to Improve the Human Condition Have Failed* (New Haven & London, Yale University Press, 1998).

[156] Shambaugh, David, *China's Communist Party: Atrophy and Adaptation* (Berkeley, University of California Press, 2008).

[157] Sharman, J. C., *Repression and Resistance in Communist Europe* (London, Routledge, 2003).

[158] Shepilov, D. T., 'Vospominaniya: antipartiinaya gruppa, kotoroi ne bylo', *Voprosy istorii*, No. 11–12, 1998, pp. 3–9.

[159] Siegelbaum, Lewis and Ronald Suny (eds), *Making Workers Soviet: Power, Class and Identity* (Ithaca, Cornell University Press, 1994).

[160] Smith, S. A., *Revolution and the People in Russia and China: A Comparative History* (Cambridge, Cambridge University Press, 2008).

[161] Snyder, Timothy, *Bloodlands: Europe Between Hitler and Stalin* (London, Bodley Head, 2010).

[162] Solzhenitsyn, Alexander, *Letter to the Soviet Leaders* (London, Collins/Harvill, 1974).

[163] Solzhenitsyn, Alexander (ed.), *From Under The Rubble* (London, Fontana/Collins, 1976).

[164] Solzhenitsyn, Alexander, *The Russian Question at the End of the Twentieth Century* (London, The Harvill Press, 1995).

[165] Solzhenitsyn, Alexander, 'Misconceptions about Russia as a Threat to America', *Foreign Affairs*, Vol. 58, No. 4, Spring 1980, pp. 797–834.

[166] Solzhenitsyn, Alexander, 'Razmyshleniya nad Fevral'skoi revolyutsiei', *Rossiiskaya gazeta*, 27 February 2007.

[167] Solzhenitsyn, Alexander, 'Napisano krov'yu', *Izvestiya*, 24 July 2007, p. 5.

[168] Sorokin, Pitirim, *A Long Journey: The Autobiography of Pitirim A. Sorokin* (New Haven, CT, College and University Press, 1963).

[169] Steinberg, Mark D., *Voices of Revolution, 1917* (New Haven and London, Yale University Press, 2001).

[170] Stojanovic, Svetozar, 'The Epochal Dilemma', in *Between Ideals and Reality* (New York, Oxford University Press, 1973).

[171] Stolypin, Petr, interview in *Volga* newspaper, 1 September 1909; in E. V[erpakhovskaya], *Gosudarstvennaya deyatel'nost' P. A. Stolypina*, Vol 1 (St Petersburg, 1909), p. 8.

[172] Suraska, Wisla, *How the Soviet Union Disappeared: An Essay on the Causes of Dissolution* (Durham and London, Duke University Press, 1998).

[173] Szamuely, Tibor, *The Russian Tradition* (London, Fontana, 1988).

[174] Talmon, J. L., *The Origins of Totalitarian Democracy* (London, Sphere Books, 1970 [1952]).

[175] Thurston, Robert W., *Liberal City, Conservative State: Moscow and Russia's Urban Crisis, 1906–1914* (Oxford, Oxford University Press, 1987).

[176] Tolz, Vera, *Russian Academicians and the Revolution: Combining Professionalism and Politics* (Basingstoke, Macmillan, 1997).

[177] Trotsky, Leon, 'Our Political Tasks' ('Nashi politicheskie zadachi') (Geneva, 1904).

[178] Trotsky, Leon, 'Bonapartism as a Regime of Crisis', in Leon Trotsky, *The Revolution Betrayed: What is the Soviet Union and Where is it Going?* (London, New Park Publications, 1973), pp. 273–9.

[179] Troyanovsky, Oleg, *The Independent*, 7 June 1993, p. 2.

[180] Tsipko, Aleksandr, 'Istoki Stalinizma', *Nauka i zhizn'*, Nos 11 and 12, 1988, and 1 and 2, 1989.

[181] Tucker, R. C., 'The Image of Dual Russia', in R. C. Tucker, *The Soviet Political Mind* (London, George, Allen & Unwin), 1972, pp. 121–42.

[182] van den Bercken, William, 'Postcommunism *avant la lettre*: Russia's Religious Thinkers on Communism in 1918', *Religion, State and Society*, Vol. 20, Nos 3–4, 1992, pp. 345–59.

[183] van der Linden, Marcel, *Western Marxism and the Soviet Union: A Survey of Critical Theories and Debates Since 1917* (Leiden, Brill, 2007).

[184] van Ree, Erik, *The Political Thought of Joseph Stalin: A Study in Twentieth Century Revolutionary Patriotism* (London, Routledge, 2002).

[185] Waldron, Peter, *Between Two Revolutions: Stolypin and the Politics of Renewal in Russia* (London, UCL Press, 1998).

[186] Walicki, Andrzej, *A History of Russian Thought: From the Enlightenment to Marxism* (Stanford, Stanford University Press, 1979).

[187] Walicki, Andrzej, *Marxism and the Leap to the Kingdom of Freedom: The Rise and Fall of the Communist Utopia* (Stanford, CA, Stanford University Press, 1995).

[188] Webb, Sidney and Beatrice Webb, *Soviet Communism, A New Civilization?*, (London, Longman, 1935; 2nd edn 1937).

[189] Weiner, Douglas, *Models of Nature: Ecology, Conservation, and Cultural Revolution in Soviet Russia* (Bloomington, IN, Indiana University Press, 1988).

[190] Wheatcroft, Stephen, 'Agency and terror: Evdokimov and Mass Killing in Stalin's Great Terror', *Australian Journal of Politics and History*, Vol. 53, No. 1, 2007, pp. 20–43.

[191] Willerton, John P., *Patronage and Politics in the USSR* (Cambridge, Cambridge University Press, 1992).

[192] Wittfogel, Karl, *Oriental Despotism: A Comparative Study of Total Power* (New Haven, Yale University Press, 1957).

[193] Yakovlev, Alexander, *Soviet Weekly*, 10 October 1991, p. 6.

[194] Yaney, George L., 'The Concept of the Stolypin Land Reform', *Slavic Review*, Vol. 23, No. 2, June 1964, pp. 275–93.

[195] Yanov, Alexander, *The Russian New Right* (Berkeley, Institute of International Studies, University of California Press, 1978).

[196] Yurchak, Alexei, *Everything Was Forever, Until It Was No More: The Last Soviet Generation* (Princeton, NJ, Princeton University Press, 2005).

[197] Zamyatin, Evgenii, *We* 1924.

[198] Zaslavsky, V. and R. Brym, 'The Function of Elections in the USSR', *Soviet Studies*, Vol. 30, No. 3, July 1978, pp. 362–71.

Index

157